Model Mysteries
An Exploration of
Vampires, Zombies and Other Fantastic
Scenarios to Make the World a Better Place

Revised Edition

Anne LaVigne and Lees Stuntz
in collaboration with the Creative Learning Exchange

CREATIVE LEARNING Exchange
Making Thinking Visible

Creative Learning Exchange
Acton, Massachusetts
2017, 2022

Dedicated to George Richardson...
our teacher, our guide and our friend

Acknowledgements

This book was created through the efforts, encouragement, and support of many and is the culmination of learning gained from years of collaboration with more people than we could possibly name. In addition to being grateful to our loving families and to each and every person who helped us along the journey, special thanks goes to those directly involved in the review, editing, and final project completion:

Brian Bindschadler   Jan Bramhall
Diana Fisher   Marcy Kenah
Bunny Lawton   George Richardson
Alan Ticotsky   Larry Weathers

Cover art of an aurora taken from space by NASA, Public Domain.

Funding was made possible through the generosity of the
GORDON BROWN FUND.

Preface

You may have heard the phrase, "Lions and tigers and bears, oh my!" voiced by Dorothy in *The Wizard of Oz* many years ago. Her problems seem small in comparison to some we're facing in today's world. Many of our problems keep repeating themselves throughout history, finding their way into our popular culture, including fictional stories. So in this era, rather than lions, tigers and bears, we might think about zombies, vampires and other fantastical scenarios, OH MY! Even though these types of situations may seem a little silly, exploring them can help increase understanding of some of those more real, difficult problems we're working to solve. So, given that...

- How can zombie chickens taking over the world be similar to a growing national debt or the possible extinction of an endangered species?
- How can the distribution of a new mind-control technology be similar to working toward a goal, like improving your grades?
- How can vampires spreading throughout a big city be similar to the spread of a new deadly disease?

These and other included explorations are about deriving helpful answers, but the REAL point is to see how the underlying system works. As an example, if we were talking about automobiles, one set of lessons is to learn how to drive a car, but another – deeper – set of instructions is how to build and maintain an automobile. In the following chapters, we are going to be looking "underneath the hood" of each model.

Also, it's important for us all to recognize that no model is ever going to be perfect, but model makers know that, and they continuously work to improve them to make them behave closer to how things work in the real world.

©Dean Alston, Used with permission

Why should you care?

Barry Richmond, creator of STELLA® software, coined the term "Systems Citizen." The term is grounded in his idea that if people increase their awareness and insights about the systems around them, they can better make logical decisions while increasing their empathy at the same time. He illustrated this point by showing an image of someone who was clearly not aware of how his actions impacted others. Chris Soderquist later wrote this definition, "Systems Citizens have empathy, they respect others, and they wish to make the world a better place for everyone."

As you use this book, your understanding of systems in general and these systems in particular will increase. If our understanding of systems expands, the hope is we'll also make decisions that result in a better world for all.

"If you can think it, you can model it."

In memory of Jay Forrester
1918-2016

Jay Forrester, founder of the field of System Dynamics, believed that the best place to foster an understanding of system dynamics was in K-12 education. One way he actualized his vision was through encouraging others to provide a focus on system dynamics in education for students ages 3 to 18. Through those connections and efforts, the Creative Learning Exchange, established by John Bemis, and the Waters Foundation, established by Jim and Faith Waters, began focusing on K-12 work.

Over the past 25 years, Jay has been an inspiration and guide as we collaborated to help students utilize the critical thinking tools of system dynamics. It has been an exciting and exhilarating journey, with all of us, Jay included, learning together to focus on what helps students learn in the most productive way. He was a mentor and a lodestone for our efforts. We were graced with the presence of a titan in our midst, and he will be sorely missed.

His brilliance and guidance will continue to inspire us as we strive to realize his vision.

Table of Contents

Getting Started

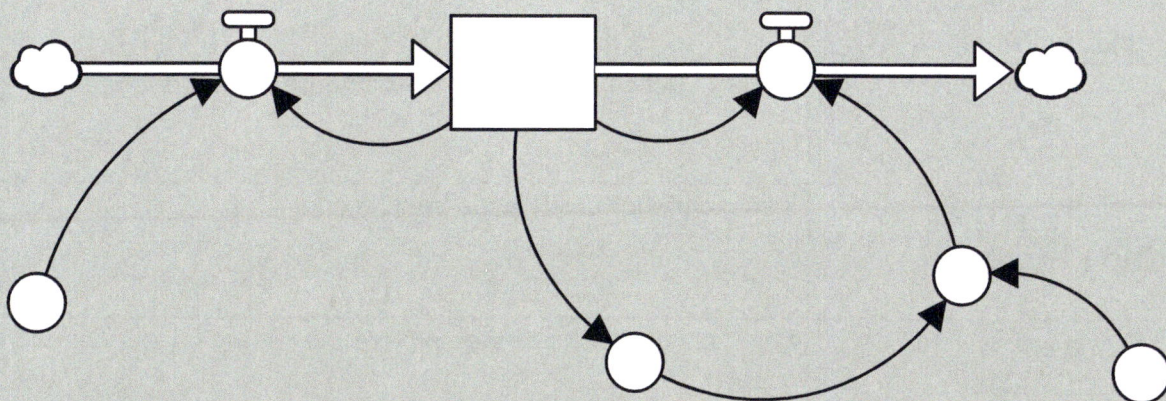

Overview

Never heard of stocks and flows? Never created models before? Don't worry about a thing. As with most new adventures, the best way to begin is to do just that. This section introduces the basics and shows how to jump in and get started.

Who can use this book?

The modeling activities are intended for students from ages 10 to 110. In other words, if you're interested in thinking about how to solve mysteries and like the idea of creating computer models and applying them to real-world problems, this book is for you. You can use it independently as a student, work with a group of students, or if you're a teacher, share it with interested students to complete a guided or independent study project.

What is included?

The book contains six main chapters, each with a new mystery to solve. Each chapter has a number of similar stories to try, depending on your interest.

Each chapter contains:

Dive in	An introduction to the mystery and some key questions to consider
Put Together the Pieces	Instructions for building the basic model
Dare to Dig Deeper	Three challenges to further explore the central mystery of each chapter
Connect to Other Stories	Your chance to choose other mysteries to solve using the same basic model

In addition to the main chapters, Chapter 7 provides an extension to build additional capacity in modeling, and Chapter 8 includes next steps, additional resources, and information about modeling software. You can also reference the Appendices for details about completing the chapter mysteries.

What do you need to start?

First, you'll need some way to create the models. Stella was used to create the models and graphics for this book, but you are free to try other options. Some options are free and some are not. Some options are online and some must be installed onto a computer or iPad. Check Appendix B for information about various modeling software options. Once you have a modeling program, you can dive into the mysteries!

As with most new endeavors, start at the beginning. The chapters are ordered from simpler to more complex concepts, so you can build your understanding as you move from one chapter to the next. If you get stuck, you can find hints about completing the chapter mysteries in the Appendix B.

Book Resources

What are the basic building blocks?

To get started with modeling, you need just four simple parts to create the model and then one more to see the results. Using these four parts, you can represent the interconnections in a system, creating something similar to a spider's web. All the strands together show the big picture of a situation. If you pull on any one strand, it can affect many other parts.

Stock

A stock represents an amount you want to track in a model. It's an accumulation. It can be concrete, like the number of trees or animals in an ecosystem or abstract, like an amount of happiness.

Bison, U.S Fish & Wildlife, Public Domain

Sunset Hopping, by Reebs, CC 3.0

Flow

Flows go into and out from stocks. The amount of "stuff" of a stock increases or decreases through one or more flows. The flow is kind of like a river flowing into or out from a lake. Some rivers flow fast, while others move very slowly. Flows work in a similar way, showing how quickly "stuff" moves in or out of a stock.

Giffre River, Wikimedia Commons, Public Domain

Converter

A converter represents part of how the system works, but it isn't a stock. For example, the number of people planting trees can be a converter.

Connector

Connectors show how elements affect one another. For example, the number of people planting trees affects the number of new seedlings in a forest.

Planting trees, NASA, Public Domain

Graph

Graphs show what happens to model elements over time. Generally, you create a graph to show what's happening to the stocks over time.

How are the instructions set up?

Each chapter contains a model you can build to help explore a mystery question. The included stock/flow diagram shows the basic structure of the model. Simply recreate the model in the modeling software of your choice.

1. Each part has a unique label.

2. Each part has a number or symbol inside. They show what you need to do to make the math work. When you actually create the model, these numbers will not appear on the diagram as they are shown in the book.

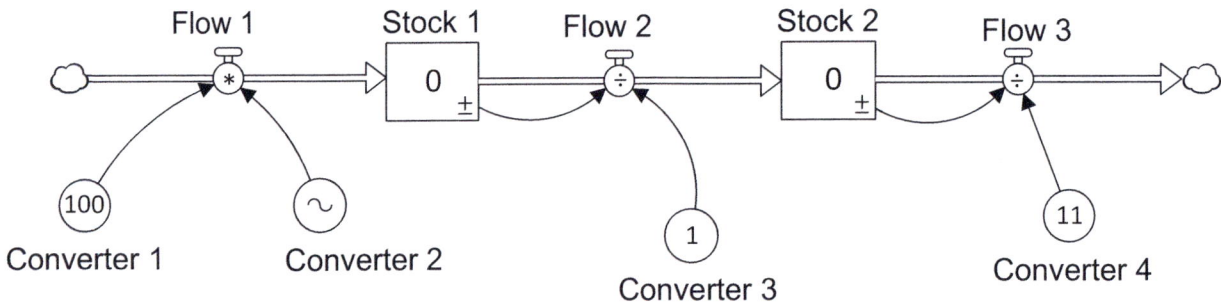

3. The symbols show math operations (+, −, *, or ÷) or a tilde sign (~), meaning that you need to create a special graph.

Then you'll create a graph with the stock (as a variable) on the y-axis and time on the x-axis. That way, you'll see what happens to that variable over a particular time period. You'll check the results to make sure that you get the correct results, and if not, adjust the model. NOTE: If you choose software other than Stella, you may see slightly different results on the graph, but the value at the end should still match.

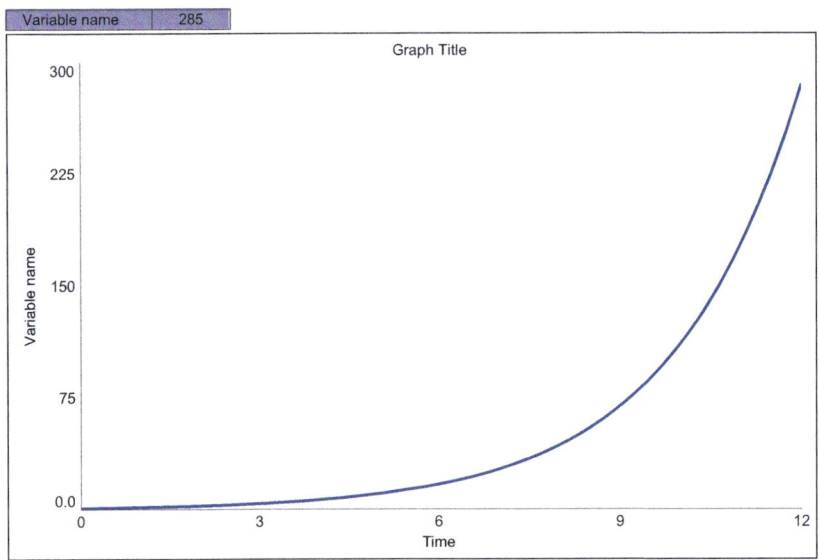

After that, you can explore other situations using the same basic model.

So, are you ready to go? Let's get started with the first mystery – how to stop the zombie chickens from over-populating Earth!

Chapter 1:
Growing, Growing, Gone

Chickens, Public Domain [modified].

Dive in – How can you stop zombie chickens from over-populating planet Earth?

Sometimes it's fun to imagine a crazy, "What if?" Like, what would happen if one day, a zombie chicken were to appear? Where that zombie chicken is from, no one knows, but now that it's here, it's trying to populate planet Earth with more and more zombie chickens.

It starts with just one zombie chicken, but that chicken grows bigger and bigger until one day, POP; now two zombie chickens stand there. The process repeats, and POP, now four zombie chickens look dazed and ready to grow.

How fast will the zombie chickens grow and pop? How can you stop it from happening?

🧩 Put Together the Pieces

First, you need some "Zombie chickens" (ZCs) and a way for them to increase (POP, i.e., replicate) and decrease (get cured). Create the following:

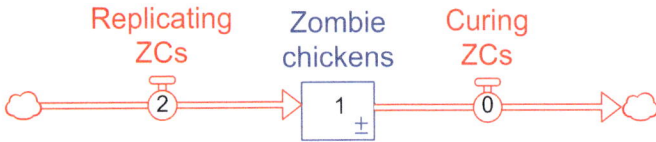

Input the numbers as indicated in the diagram.
See Appendix B: Equation Helper for assistance if needed.

Set up the model's "Run Specs" as follows:
   Start Time = 0
   Stop Time = 12
   DT = 0.25 or 1/4
   Time Units = Months
   Integration Method = Euler

Also make sure that the stock is set to allow negative values. In other words, if you are using Stella software, you must un-check the "Non-negative" box in the settings for each stock you create.

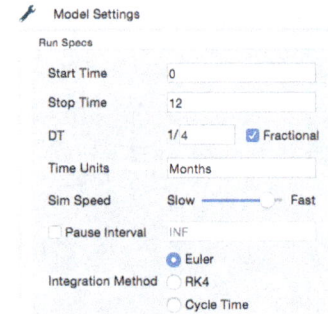

Create a graph of ZCs. Run the model to see what happens. If all the initial values are correctly entered, you should see the following graph line and ending numerical value. You may need to set the graph's scale to match the one below.

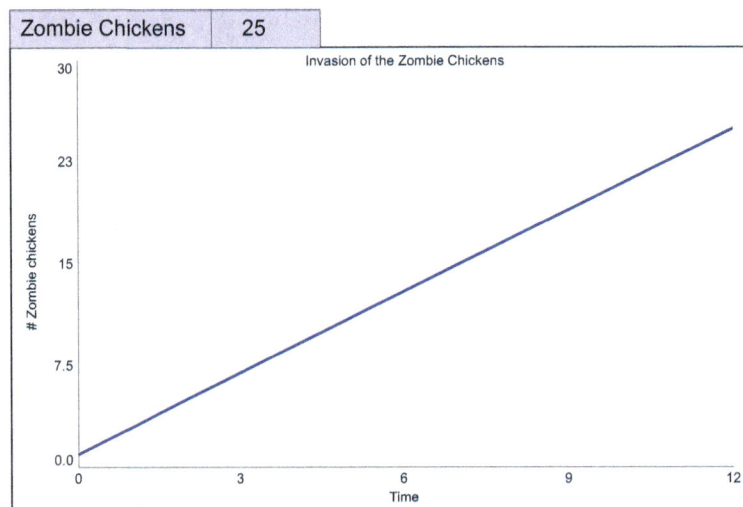

If the behavior is different, recheck your connections and equations. If the behavior is still not matched, check Appendix B: Equation Helper for guidance.

Experiment, changing the numbers for ZCs, replicating ZCs and curing ZCs to see how it affects the number of ZCs over time. Change only one number for each run. You should see variations similar to the graph lines shown here.

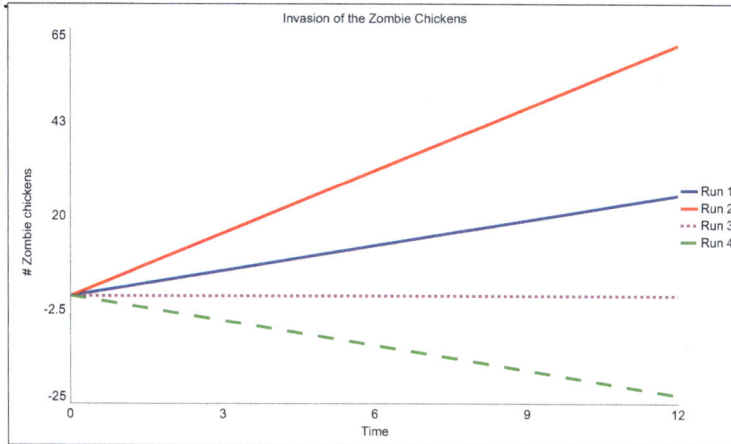

Notice that no matter what numbers you input, the ZCs grow, decline or stay the same in a straight line. That doesn't quite match the situation of one becoming two, two becoming four and so on. Another issue is that the model allows for a negative number of ZCs, which of course, is not possible. This means that the model structure is wrong; it needs to be adjusted to prevent this impossibility.

Add a little more to your model and adjust the equations. The arrows coming out from the stock of ZCs to the flows show that the number of ZCs affects how many go in or come out. NOTE: The $*$ symbol means to multiply the variables that affect that part.

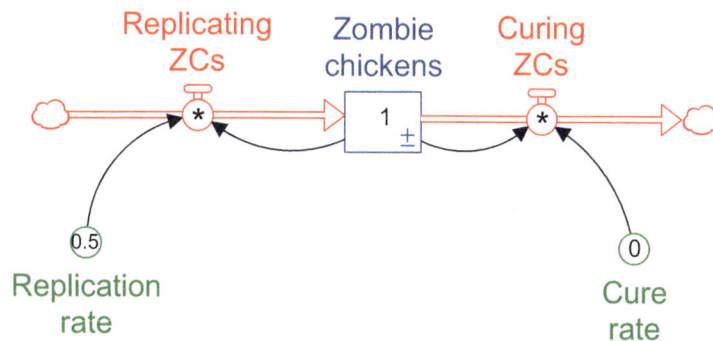

Run the model to see what happens. If all the initial values are correctly entered, you should see the following graph line and ending numerical value. Notice that the line is now curved, so the ZCs are increasing faster over time. If the behavior is different, recheck your connections and equations. Note that although the model has a way to cure ZCs, the number is currently set to 0, so no ZCs are cured.

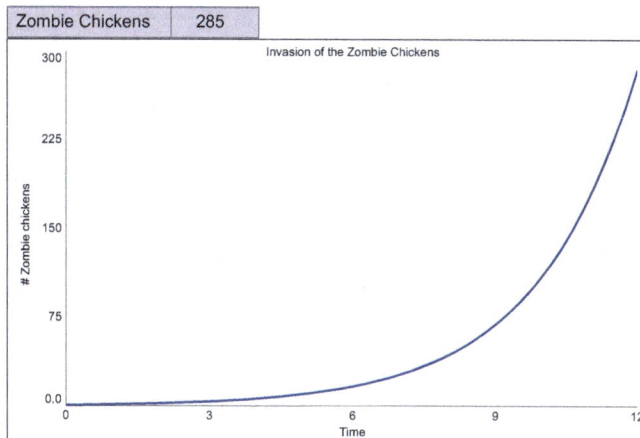

Dare to Dig Deeper

Dare yourself to find solutions using the model you created. Some key questions to dig into are:
1. How long would it take before the number of ZCs outnumber the number of people on Earth?
2. Is it possible to stop the invasion? What would be necessary to reverse the trend? How might a cure help solve the problem?

D Dare

1. Keeping the numbers the same, how many months will it take for the ZCs to outnumber the number of people on Earth? To keep the model simple, let's assume that the human population stays the same. At the revision of this book, the population was nearly eight billion people. Hint: You'll need to change the number of months the model runs.
2. Sketch the graph and then compare it to the graph in Appendix B: Equation Helper.

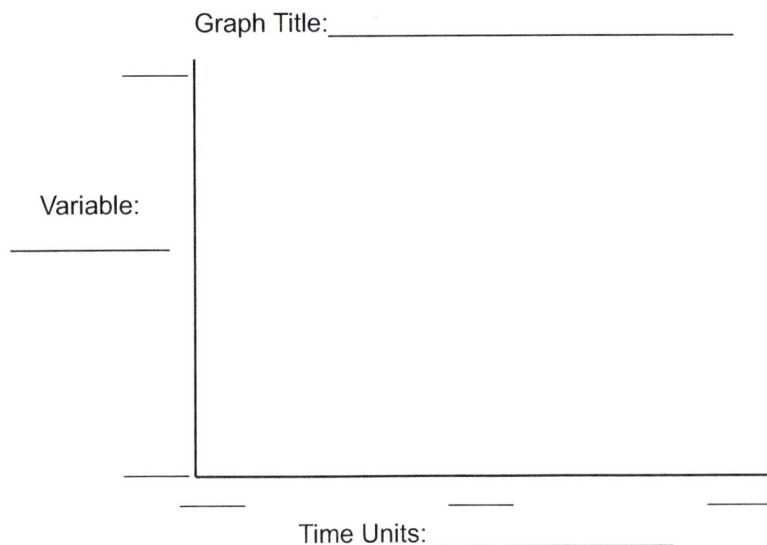

Graph Title:_____

Variable:
_____

Time Units:_____

D Double Dare

1. Think about what is needed to prevent the ZCs from taking over the Earth. Up to this point, the cure rate is set at 0. This means that no ZCs are changed back into regular chickens. What do you predict will happen if the "Cure rate" is set to 25% cured per month? The setting would be 0.25.
2. Try different numbers for the "Cure rate" to determine what is needed to prevent the zombie takeover.

D Triple Dog Dare

1. In reality, it would take time to develop a cure. Given that, will it still be possible to stop the ZCs in time to save the Earth?
2. Change the equation for "Cure rate" to show the time it takes to develop the cure.
   - The equation for "Cure rate" is: STEP(0.5,10). This means that it takes 10 months to develop a cure. No ZCs will be cured from months 0-9. Starting in month 10, you'll cure 50% (0.5) of the ZCs per month.
   - What do you predict will happen to the number of ZCs over time?
   - Try some different ideas, changing only one number at a time. Sketch your best graph, showing how to eliminate the ZCs.

Graph Title:_____

Variable:
_____

Time Units:_____

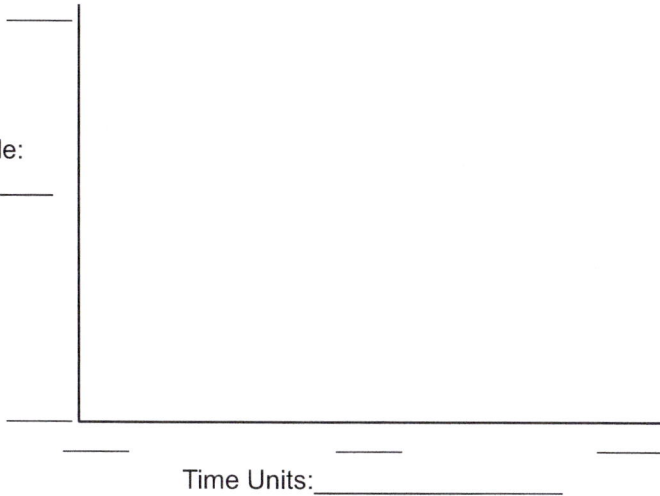

Reflect
What did you change to create this result?

Dare to Reflect:

Think about the changes that were most effective and also realistic in solving the ZC problem. For example, if you develop a cure, consider whether you gave a reasonable amount of time for the cure to be created and put into place.

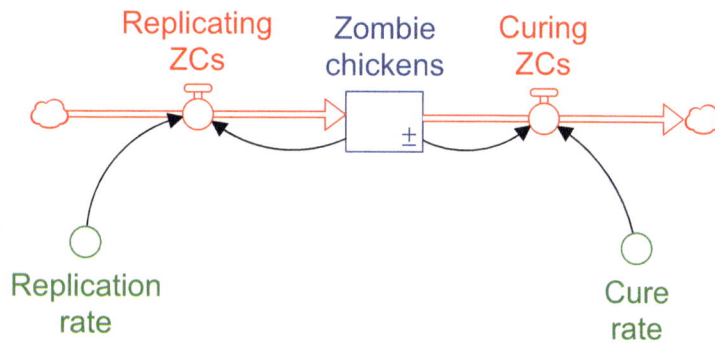

Thoughts and Insights from this Model:

Connect to Other Stories

Many other situations (real and fictional) behave in a similar way as this simple model does. Modify the labels and numbers for the zombie chicken model to explore one or more of these stories. You can even make up your own stories that have behaviors similar to those seen in this model.

Story 1: Dodo Disappearance
Overview
In the 1600s, the dodo, a type of bird went extinct. Use this model to consider the basics of why this animal became extinct and how that extinction might have been stopped.

Details
1. Time units_____
2. Dodos (stock)_____
3. Birth fraction_____
4. Death fraction_____

Dodo, by Christian Friedrich Stölze. Public Domain

D Dare

1. Re-label and change the numbers in the previous model to make sense for this situation.
2. Determine how long it would take for the population of dodos to disappear.

D Double Dare

1. Using the model, think of at least two ways to slow down the decline of the dodos.
2. Choose one idea and change the number for that part in the model to achieve slower decline. Remember that the only ways to affect the number of dodos is by affecting the number of births or the number of deaths. Make sure that your number is realistic.
3. Try some different ideas, changing only one number at a time. Sketch your best graph.

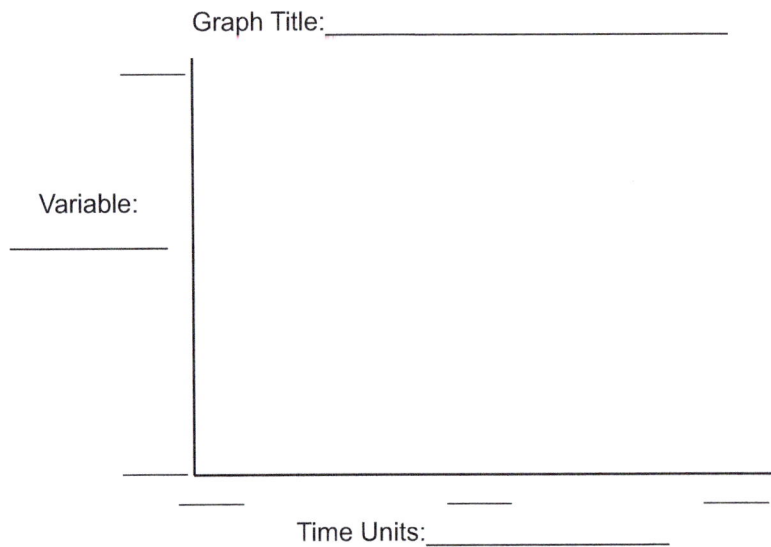

Graph Title:_____

_____

Variable:
_____

Time Units:_____

Reflect
What did you change to create this result?

D Triple Dog Dare

1. Can you add something to the model to show a new plan to save the dodos? Perhaps a new law limits how many are hunted, or maybe a breeding program is implemented.
2. What could you do to increase the number of dodos rather than having them go extinct?

Story 2: National Debt
Overview

The United States (and some other countries) have borrowed money to pay for government programs. This borrowed money is called the National Debt. Every year the debt goes up based on the deficit (the new money borrowed each year) and the interest being charged on the existing debt. Each year, payments are made, but it hasn't been enough to reduce the actual debt. You can see the current debt here: https://fiscaldata.treasury.gov/americas-finance-guide/national-debt/. As of November 2022, the debt is more than $31 trillion. Do some research to determine logical values for the model's details.

Details

1. Time units_____
2. National debt (stock)_____
3. Amount added (deficit) per time unit_____
4. Amount paid per time unit_____
5. Interest rate_____

National Debt sign, Jesper Rautell Balle, Creative Commons 3.0

D Dare

1. Re-label and change the numbers in the previous model to make sense for this situation.
2. Given the current pattern, how much will the debt be in 2050?

D Double Dare

1. Using the model, think of at least two ways to slow the accumulation of debt.
2. Choose one idea and change the number for that part in the model to achieve slower growth. Make sure that your number is realistic, that is, consider that if you cut spending, you are actually cutting government programs, such as military personnel, aid to low income families, and subsidized farming.
3. Try some different ideas, changing only one number at a time. Sketch your best graph.

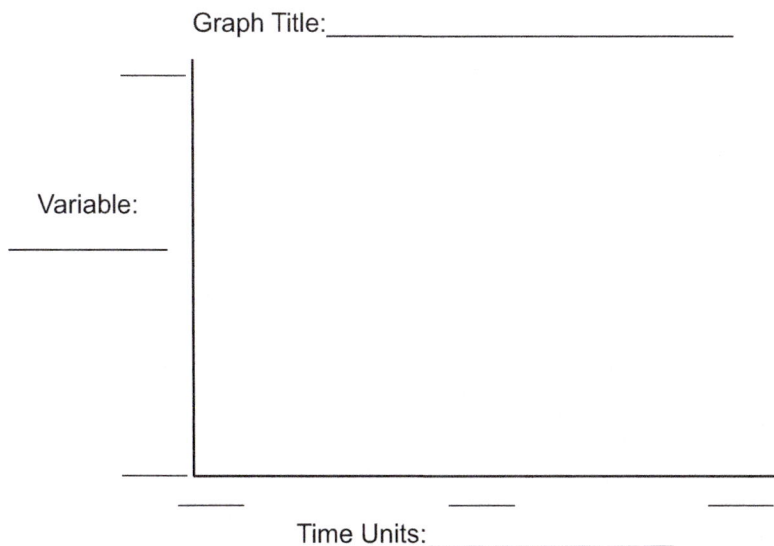

Graph Title:_____

_____

Variable:

_____

Time Units:_____

Reflect
What did you change to create this result?

D Triple Dog Dare

1. Can you add something to the model to show a new plan to decrease the debt? Make sure that your additions are realistic.

Story 3: Interested in Interest
Overview

You want to save money for college. Consider how much you will need each year for tuition and living expenses. Adjust the time frame to run for the amount of time you have to save between now and when you graduate from high school.

Details

1. Time units_____
2. Money (stock)_____
3. Deposits per time unit_____
4. Interest rate earned_____

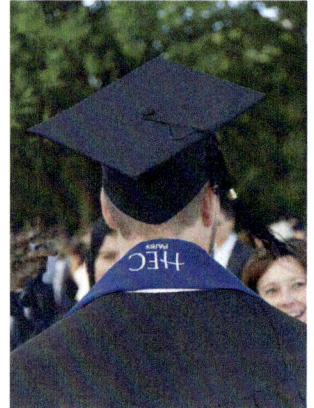

Graduation, Paris, Public Domain

D Dare

1. Re-label and change the numbers in the previous model to make sense for saving for college.
2. Given your current saving rate, how much will you have by the time you graduate from high school?

D Double Dare

1. Reconsider your saving rate in order to determine a plan to save the total amount needed. Using the model, think of at least two ways to increase the amount saved.
2. Choose one idea and change the number for that part in the model to achieve faster growth. Make sure that your number is possible, that is, you can realistically save that amount of money in the time between now and your high school graduation.
3. Try some different ideas, changing only one number at a time. Sketch your best graph.

Graph Title:_____

Variable:
_____

Time Units:_____

Reflect
What did you change to create this result?

D Triple Dog Dare

1. Can you add something to the model to show a new plan to increase your savings? Make sure that your additions are realistic.

Story 4: Your Story
Create your own story with details, using an issue that behaves in a similar way. Modify the model to match your story, and use it to solve the problem(s).

Dare to Reflect:
One story I tried was_____

How did you adjust the model to solve the problem(s)? Create labels for the diagram and add any new part(s).

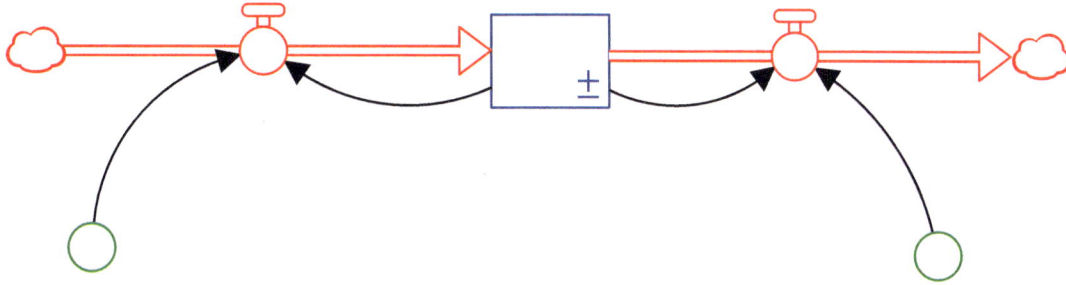

What would these model adjustments actually mean is happening in the real world?

Other thoughts and insights:

Chapter 2:
Energy Drink Mania

Energy drink cans, Mark J Merry, Creative Commons 2.0. [cropped version]

🐸 Dive in – How does your body process energy drinks?

Have you heard? Sleep is out of fashion. It's time to wake up and stay awake for as long as you can. You might have heard the phrase "burning the candle at both ends," meaning that people are trying to stay up late and get up early too, just to keep up with everything they need to get done.

Energy drinks have created a way to accomplish this, but with costs, of course. This chapter does not address those costs – financial, physical or mental. It does show one basic result of ingesting energy drinks – raising the level of caffeine in the body.

🧩 Put Together the Pieces

First, you need two stocks, one for "Mg caffeine in stomach" and another for "Mg caffeine in body." Note that Mg stands for milligrams. Energy drinks are consumed, land in the stomach, are absorbed by the body, and are eventually eliminated[1]. Create the following:

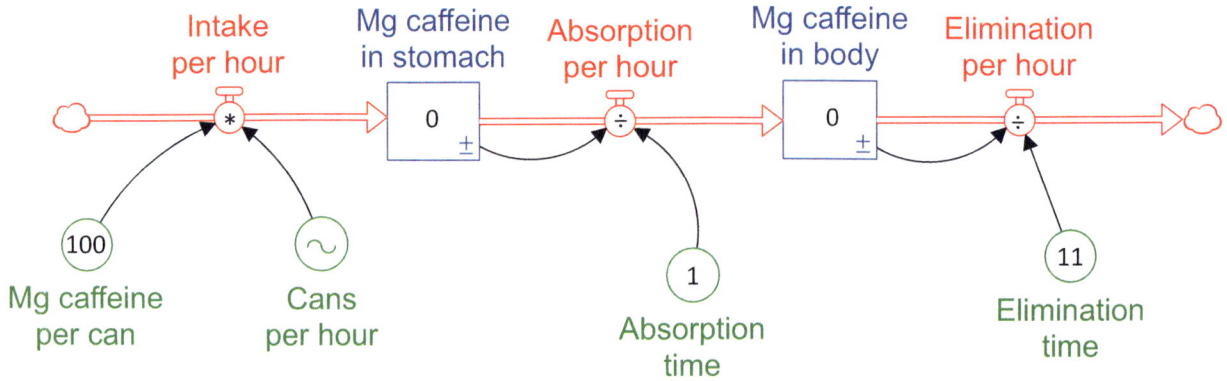

Input the numbers and equations as indicated in the diagram. See Appendix B: Equation Helper for assistance if needed. Note that "Cans per hour" has a tilde sign (~) and needs a special equation called a graphical function. A graphical function allows you to decide when the individual will and won't be consuming energy drinks over an entire 24-hour period. The details for this are below.

Set up the model's "Run Specs" as follows:

Start Time = 0
Stop Time = 24
DT = 0.25 or 1/4
Time Units = Hours
Integration Method = Euler

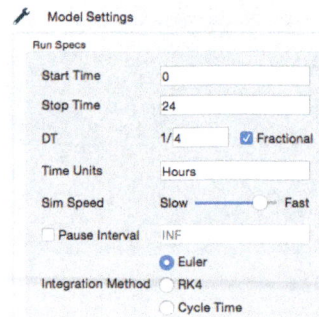

Create the graphical function:
1. Type TIME as the equation for "Cans per hour."
2. Click on the function ⌂ icon.
3. Check the box for "Graphical."
4. Set the y-axis scale to be 0-2 "Cans per hour" and the x-axis to be 0-24 "Time," with time being hours in a day.
5. Create the line on the graph as shown, indicating that the person drinks no energy drinks for hours 0-3, drinks one can per hour for hours 4-7, and goes back to zero cans per hour starting at hour 8.

Also make sure that the stock is set to allow negative values. In other words, if you are using Stella software, you must un-check the "Non-negative" box for each stock you create.

x^2 ⬚ Mg caffeine in body
Options
☐ Non-negative

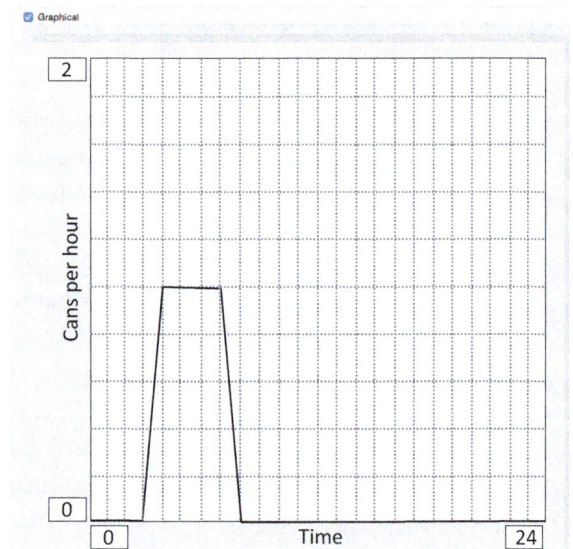

---

1 Elimination time obtained from http://www.caffeineinformer.com/the-half-life-of-caffeine

Create a graph of "Caffeine in stomach" and "Caffeine in body". Run the model to see what happens. If all the initial values are correctly entered, you should see the following graph lines and ending numerical value. You may need to set the graph's scale to match the one below.

Mg caffeine in stomach	0.00	Mg caffeine in body	82.64

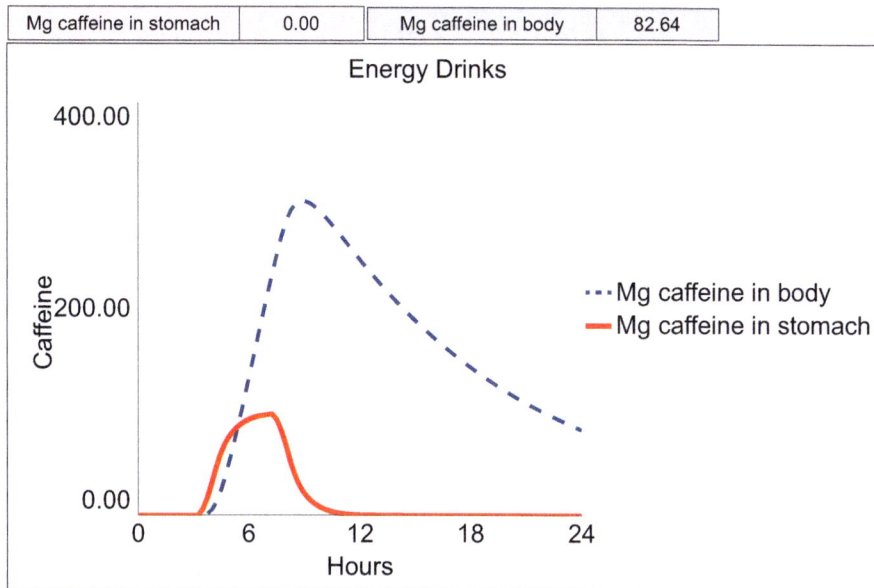

If the behavior is different, recheck your connections and equations. If the behavior is still not matched, check Appendix B: Equation Helper for guidance.

Experiment, changing the numbers for "Mg caffeine per can" and the graph line for "Cans per hour" to see how it affects the amount of caffeine in the body over time[2]. Change only one variable for each run. Use the table below as a guide for changing "Mg caffeine per can." These are meant to show a selection of energy drinks with a range of caffeine amounts, but feel free to look up additional brands.[3]

Energy Drink	Size (in ounces)	Milligrams Caffeine
Archer Farms Energy Drink	12	100
Cola (typical brands)	12	40
Jolt Cola Energy Drink	23.5	280
Monster Energy Drink	16	160
Red Bull	8.46	80
Rock Star Sparkling Energy	16	160
10 Hour Energy Shot	1.93	422

---

2 This model is not intended to predict exact amounts of caffeine in any individual's body or to provide a guide for the maximum number of drinks to safely consume. The model, like all others can show general trends, but is by its nature, not an exact match for reality. It also does not take into account differences in age or weight.
3 Energy drink caffeine amounts obtained from http://www.caffeineinformer.com/the-caffeine-database

Try some variations for the "Cans per hour" graphical function and compare results.

Option 1

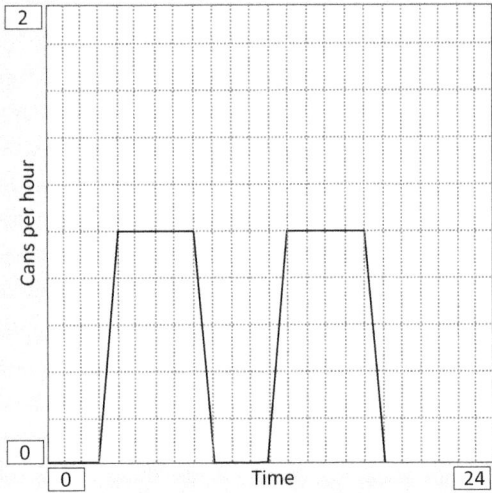

What is the drinking pattern? What happens as a result?

Option 2

☑ Graphical

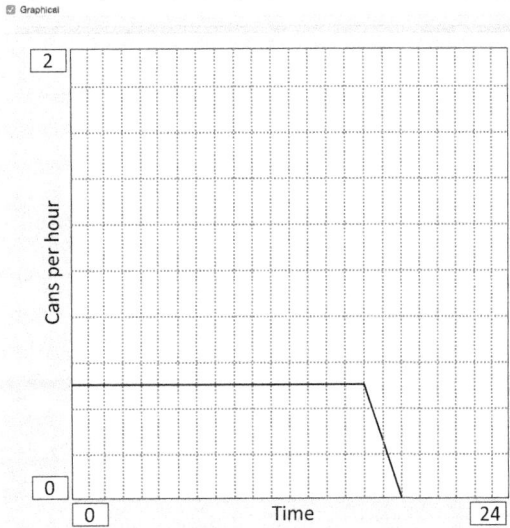

What is the drinking pattern? What happens as a result?

Option 3

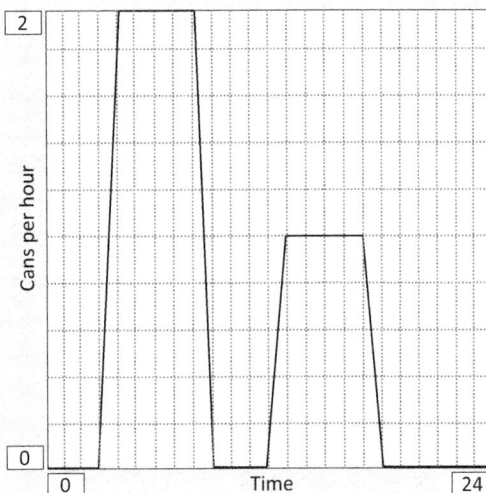

What is the drinking pattern? What happens as a result?

🔨 Dare to Dig Deeper

Dare yourself to find solutions, using the model you created to help. Key questions to dig into are:
1. How long does it take to eliminate caffeine from the body?
2. Based on consumption, what are caffeine levels in the body over time?
3. What should you consider when deciding on consumption of caffeine in energy drinks?

D Dare

1. Given the original settings, how long does it take for the caffeine to be mostly eliminated with less than 10 mg remaining in the body.
2. Sketch the graph.

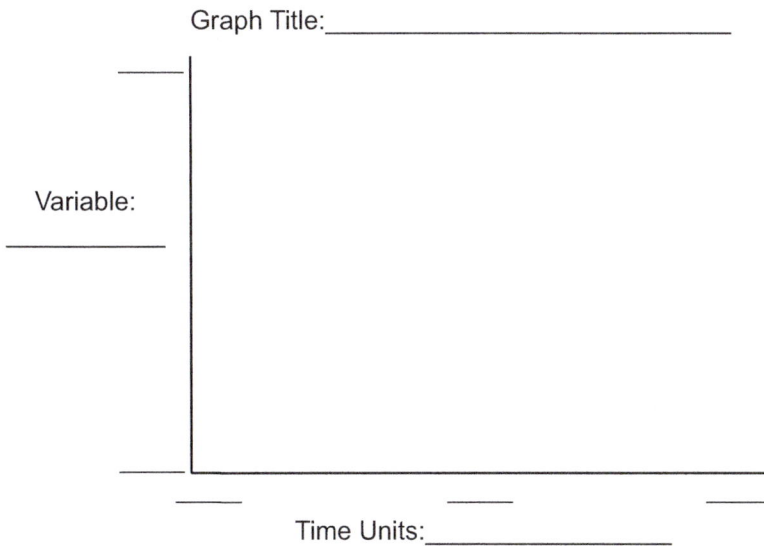

Graph Title:_____

Variable:
_____

Time Units:_____

D Double Dare

1. Think about a situation in which a person wishes to remain alert for 16 hours and then feel tired enough to sleep well at night. Using the model, what is the maximum caffeine s/he should consume in order for levels to drop below 50 mg before going to bed?

   Consider recommended caffeine amounts[4] for children, teens, and adults. Although rare, there are documented deaths from caffeine overdoses. For healthy adults, this would be a lot of energy drinks (perhaps dozens of cans that add up to thousands of milligrams caffeine consumed), but for younger people or people with health issues, a lethal dose can be much lower[5].

Age	Recommended Maximum Daily Caffeine intake (in Mg)
12 and under	50 (although none is more desirable)
13-17	100
18 and over (healthy adult)	200-400

---

4 Recommended caffeine information from http://www.caffeineinformer.com/caffeine-safe-limits
5 Documented deaths by caffeine, http://www.caffeineinformer.com/a-real-life-death-by-caffeine

2. Try some different ideas, and then sketch your best graph.

Graph Title:_____

Variable:
_____

Time Units:_____

Reflect
What did you change to create this result?

D Triple Dog Dare

1. What are the maximum number of energy drinks a person can consume without having the caffeine level in the body go over 400 mg at any given moment?

Dare to Reflect:
Think about the changes that were most effective and also realistic in deciding on caffeine intake. For example, if someone drinks energy drinks now, is it reasonable that they would totally give them up?

Thoughts and Insights from this Model:

Connect to Other Stories

Many other situations (real and fictional) behave in a similar way as this simple model does. Modify the labels and numbers for the energy drink model to explore one or more of these stories. You can even make up your own stories that have behaviors similar to those seen in this model.

Story 1: Tree Disappearance
Overview
In a local forest, trees are planted by foresters and harvested by lumberjacks. The trees take years to grow from immature saplings to mature trees ready for harvest. The problem is that the number of trees has been declining. Use this model to consider the basics of how the trees grow, mature, are harvested as well as how to create a healthy forest over time.

Details
1. Time units_____
2. Cutting rate_____
3. Saplings (stock)_____
4. Number of foresters_____
5. Mature trees (stock)_____
6. Trees planted per forester_____
7. Time to mature_____

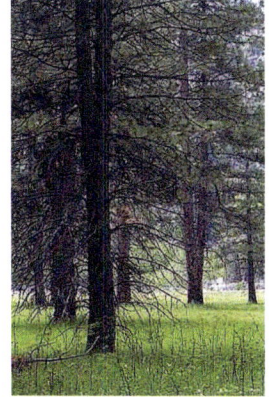

Forest, by Jon Sullivan, Public Domain

D Dare

1. Re-label and change the numbers in the previous model to make sense for this situation. Make sure to show a scenario in which the trees are declining.
2. Determine how long it would take for the trees to disappear.

D Double Dare

1. Using the model, think of at least two ways to slow the decline of the trees, ideally creating a stable number of trees over time.
2. Choose one idea and change the number for that part in the model to achieve slower decline. Make sure that your number is realistic. Sketch your best graph.

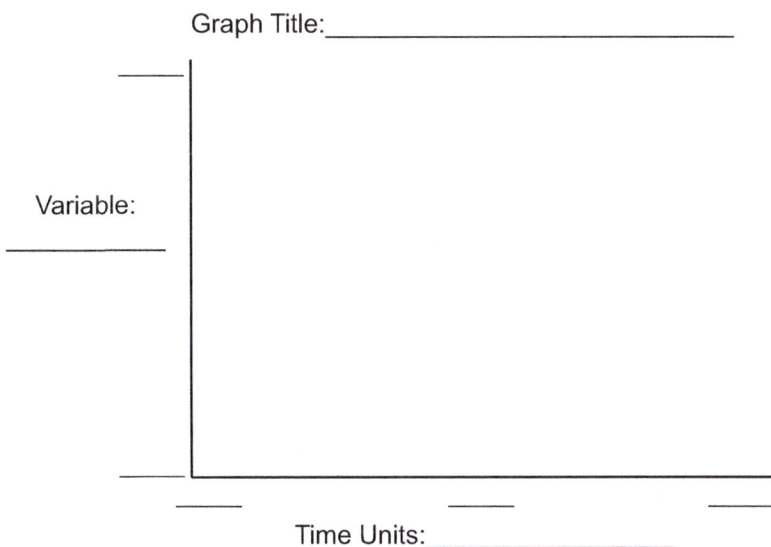

Graph Title:_____

Variable:
_____

_____

Time Units:_____

Reflect
What did you change to create this result?

D Triple Dog Dare

1. Can you add something to the model to show how the forest has a limited amount of space and still show a scenario that stops the forest from declining? You'll need to show that when the space runs out, the foresters stop planting as many trees.

Story 2: Hungry Sheep on the Commons
Overview

A small town has a commons, a large grassy area, where local farmers can bring their sheep to graze. The grass grows and the grass is eaten by the sheep. This is great for the farmers, since their sheep get free food and great for the town, since the area is naturally maintained by the grazing sheep. However, there's a problem. The grass is becoming sparse over time. Use this model to consider the basics of how the grass grows and is eaten by the sheep.

Details

1. Time units_____
2. Mature grass (stock)_____
3. Grass sprouts (stock)_____
4. Spreading new seed_____
5. Time to sprout_____
6. Eating rate_____
7. Time to grow_____

Sheep, Public Domain

D Dare

1. Re-label and change the numbers in the previous model to make sense for this situation. Make sure to show a scenario in which the grass is declining.
2. Determine how long it would take for the grass to disappear.

D Double Dare

1. Using the model, think of at least two ways to slow the decline of the grass, ideally creating a stable amount of grass over time.
2. Choose one idea and change the number for that part in the model to achieve slower decline. Make sure that your number is realistic. Sketch your best graph.

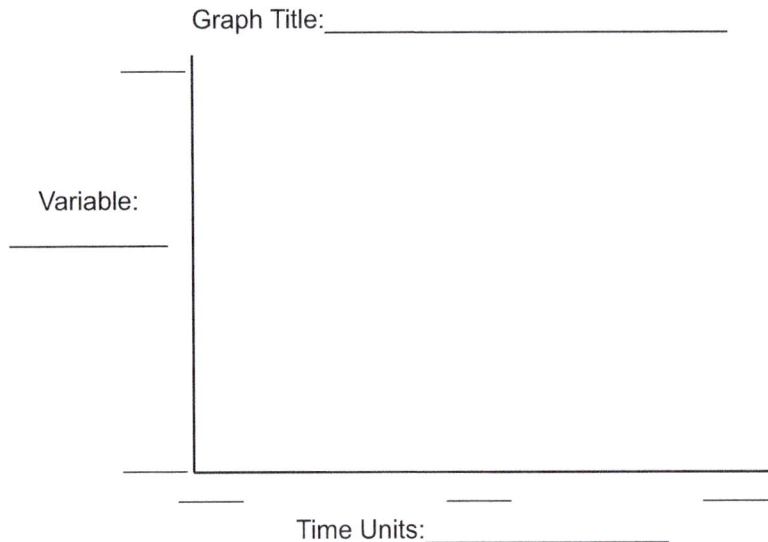

Graph Title:_____

_____

Variable:
_____

Time Units:_____

Reflect
What did you change to create this result?

D Triple Dog Dare

1. Add an element to show that the space to plant grass is limited while still keeping the grass levels high. Also consider adding sheep and a maximum amount each sheep can eat.

Story 3: Medicine Levels in the Body
Overview
In a hospital, doctors are working to get the correct dosage of medicine to a patient. It's important that the drug be delivered so that the levels remain stable in the blood. The doctors are using a time-release oral medication that takes about two hours to move from the stomach into the rest of the body. Use the model to consider how often the patient needs to take the medicine in order to maintain a level between 200-400 mg in the body by the end of day 2.

Details
1. Time units_____
2. Mg drug per pill_____
3. Drug in stomach (stock)_____
4. Pills per day_____
5. Drug in body (stock)_____
6. Elimination time_____
7. Absorption time_____

Taking a Pulse, Amanda Mills, USCDCP, Public Domain

D Dare

1. Re-label and change the numbers in the previous model to make sense for this situation.
2. Determine the best plan for "Pills per day" to achieve the correct levels in the body.

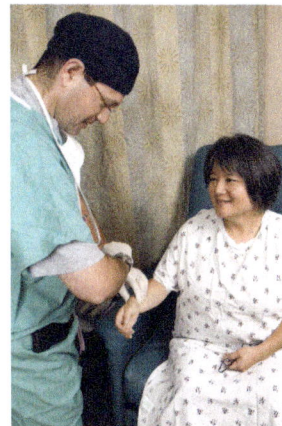

D Double Dare

1. Using the model, think of at least two ways to increase how quickly the medication reaches the correct level.
2. Choose one idea and change the number for that part in the model to achieve the correct level more quickly. Make sure that your number is realistic. Sketch your best graph.

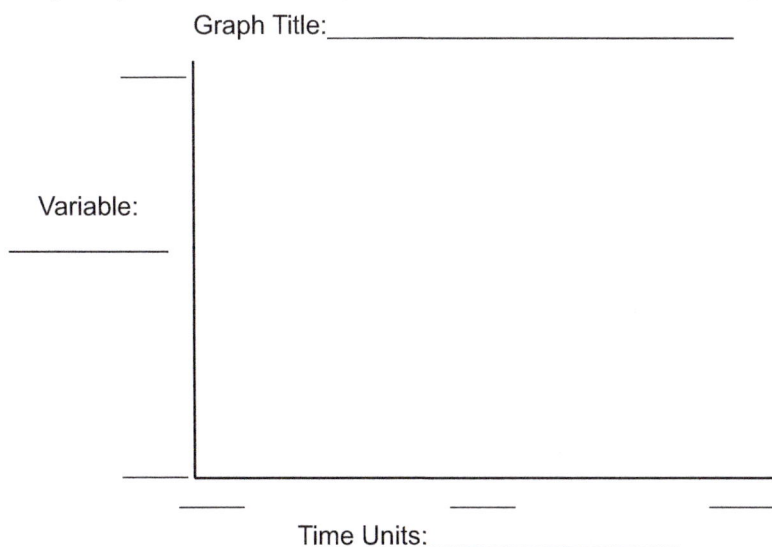

Graph Title:_____

Variable:
_____

Time Units:_____

Reflect
What did you change to create this result?

D Triple Dog Dare

1. Change the model to show how to best maintain therapeutic drug levels over the course of a week.

Story 4: Your Story

Create your own story with details, using an issue that behaves in a similar way. Modify the model to match your story, and use it to solve the problem(s).

Dare to Reflect:

One story I tried was_____

How did you adjust the model to solve the problem(s)? Create labels for the diagram and add any new part(s).

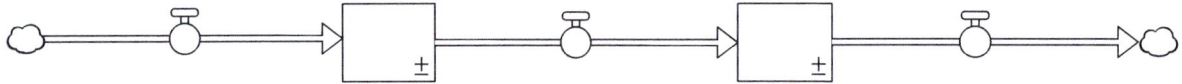

What would these model adjustments actually mean is happening in the real world?

Other thoughts and insights:

Chapter 3:
Mind the Gap

Pierneef, J.H. in Wêreldspektrum. 1983 Ensiklopedie Afrikana, Public Domain

Dive in – Can you stop evil Vic Schuss from taking over the world with his new device?

Gaps are present anytime there's a goal to accomplish something, whether that be for good or evil. A gap, in this case, is simply the difference between the desired goal and the way things are now.

In a parallel universe, Vic Schuss has designed a new personal communication device. He is working to get people to wear them, and even gives them away. His plan is to use the devices to control the actions of others, thus creating a world in which he is in charge.

Explore how long it would take him to reach his goal and what might be done to stop him.

🧩 Put Together the Pieces

First, you need a stock of "Production capacity" to show how many devices Vic Schuss can produce each week. Add a flow going in. The one drawn below is called a biflow, which is not really needed for this model, but is often needed for other similar models.

Vic Schuss needs to increase the ability of his factories to produce the new device, but that takes time. In the model, this "Time to ramp up production" is, on average, 52 weeks. His current "Production capacity" is 10,000 devices per week. He has a goal of increasing that to 1,000,000 devices per week, so he can distribute them throughout the world as quickly as possible[6]. As soon as everyone has a device, he can turn on the mind control switch and dictate the direction of world. Create the following:

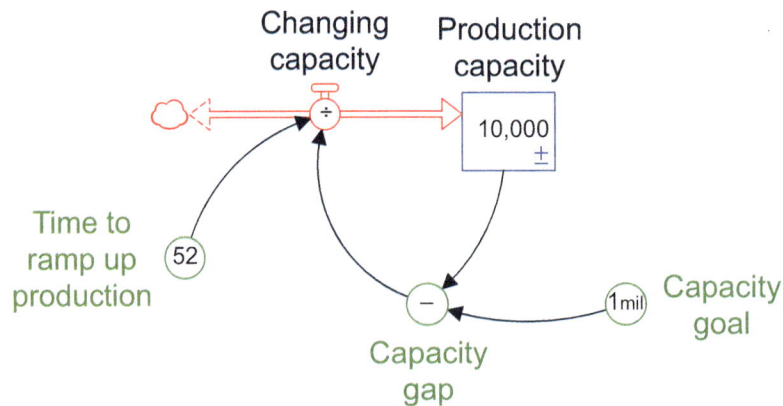

Input the numbers and equations as indicated in the diagram.
See Appendix B: Equation Helper for assistance if needed.
Set up the model's "Run Specs" as follows:

    Start Time = 0
    Stop Time = 12 weeks
    DT = 0.25 or 1/4
    Time Units = Weeks
    Integration Method = Euler

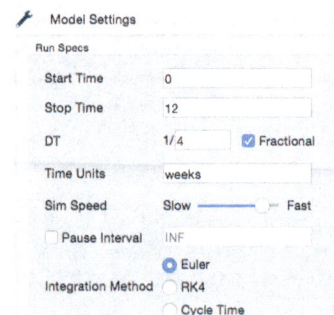

Also make sure that the stock is set to allow negative values. In other words, if you are using Stella software, you must un-check the "Non-negative" box for each stock you create.

---

6 This mystery was inspired by a plot line for a popular British television show, *Doctor Who*. Several episodes featured a device called an EarPod that could be used by its makers to control the minds of those who wore them.

Create a graph of "Production capacity." Run the model to see what happens. If all the initial values are correctly entered, you should see the following graph line and ending numerical value. You may need to set the graph's scale to match the one below.

Production capacity	214k

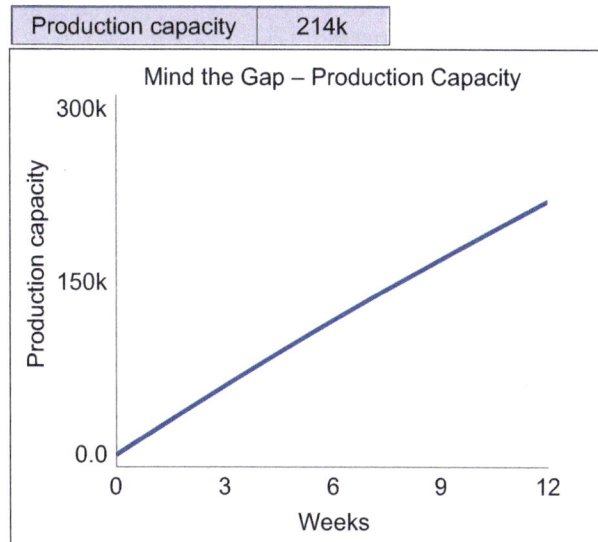

Mind the Gap – Production Capacity

If the behavior is different, recheck your connections and equations. If the behavior is still not matched, check Appendix B: Equation Helper for guidance.

Experiment, changing the numbers for "Capacity goal" and "Time to ramp up capacity" to see what happens. Change only one variable for each run.

🔨 Dare to Dig Deeper

Dare yourself to find solutions, using the model you created to help. Key questions to dig into are:
1. How long would it take Vic Schuss to reach his goal?
2. What options do you have to stop him, i.e., what leverage do you have in this situation?"

D Dare

1. Given the original settings, how long does it take for Vic Schuss to reach his goal of having a "Production capacity" of 1,000,000 devices? You'll need to extend how long the model runs.
2. Sketch the graph.

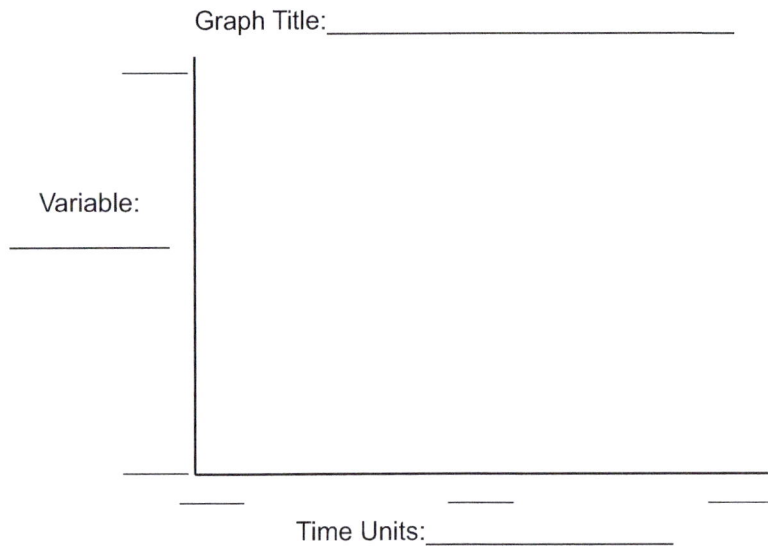

Graph Title:_____

Variable:
_____

Time Units:_____

D Double Dare

1. Imagine that a small group of people try to stop Vic Schuss. What would they need to do to prevent the production of devices? Use the model to explore what variable is leverage. Then explain what the implications of this are for real-world action.
2. Try some different ideas, and then sketch your best graph.

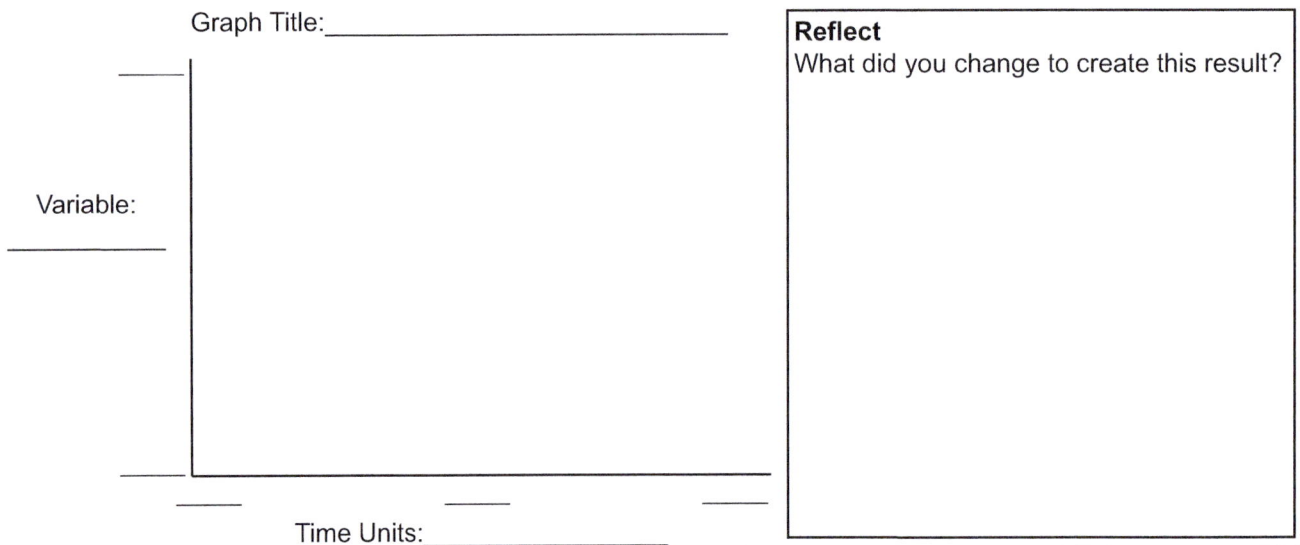

Graph Title:_____

Variable:
_____

Time Units:_____

Reflect
What did you change to create this result?

Triple Dog Dare

1. Add to the model to show how many people actually have the device. Consider that there are almost eight billion people on Earth, but also consider whether he needs to distribute the devices to everyone or just to a small percent of key individuals. What percent would he need? You'll need a second structure similar to the first and a way to show how many devices are actually available for distribution. The "Production capacity" stock should affect how many devices are available and consequently how many people actually receive them.
2. Consider leverage to stop Vic Schuss. How could you stop the production and/or distribution of the devices?

Dare to Reflect:

Think about the changes that were most effective and also realistic in deciding on a plan to stop Vic Schuss.

Thoughts and Insights from this Model:

Connect to Other Stories

Many other situations (real and fictional) behave in a similar way as this simple model does. Modify the labels and numbers for the gap model to explore one or more of these stories. You can even make up your own stories that have behaviors similar to those seen in this model.

Story 1: Gaping Grade Gap
Overview

Janey has low grades in math, and she wants to improve them. She currently has an F with a 33% average. She has a goal to improve to an A with at least a 90% average. Use the model to consider how long it would take her to improve.

Details

1. Time units_____
2. Current % (stock) _____
3. Desired %_____
4. Time to improve_____

My Math Grade – Can I Raise it from an F to an A?

Grades, A.LaVigne

D Dare

1. Re-label and change the numbers in the previous model to make sense for this situation. Make sure to show a realistic scenario in which Janey's grades are improving.
2. Determine how long it would take for Janey to raise her grade from an F to an A.

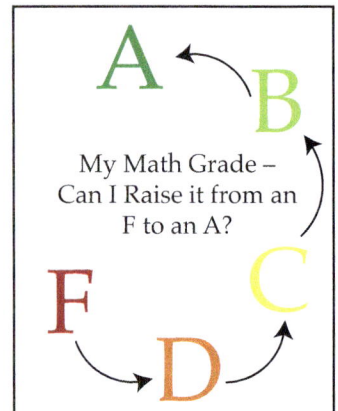

D Double Dare

1. Using the model, think of at least two ways to speed up Janey's improvement.
2. Choose one idea and change the number for that part in the model to achieve a faster improvement. Make sure that your number is realistic. Sketch your best graph.

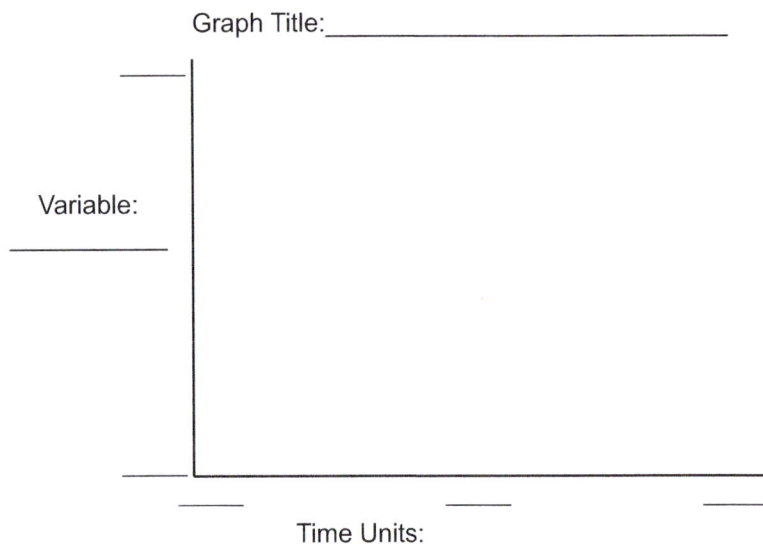

Graph Title:_____

_____

Variable:

_____

Time Units:_____

Reflect
What did you change to create this result?

D Triple Dog Dare

1. Can you add something to the model to show two gaps? Note – one gap is Janey's "Capacity to understand" the material, and the other gap is her actual grade expressed as "Current percent." You'll need two stocks, each with its own gap. Make sure that the understanding stock impacts the grade stock.

Story 2: Dreaming of the Olympics
Overview

Jon, a long-distance runner, is working hard to make the next Olympic team. He wants to improve how much time it takes him to run a mile. His current time is 6 minutes per mile. His goal is to get down to 4 minutes per mile.

Details

1. Time units_____
2. Current distance max (stock)_____
3. Desired distance max_____
4. Time to change ability_____

Runner, Wikimedia Commons, Public Domain

D Dare

1. Re-label and change the numbers in the previous model to make sense for this situation. Make sure to show a scenario in which the capacity to run is going up.
2. Determine how long it would take for the runner to run 26 miles if he can only run 5 miles to begin.

D Double Dare

1. Using the model, think of at least two ways to speed up the runner's ability.
2. Choose one idea and change the number for that part in the model to achieve faster gains. Make sure that your number is realistic. Sketch your best graph.

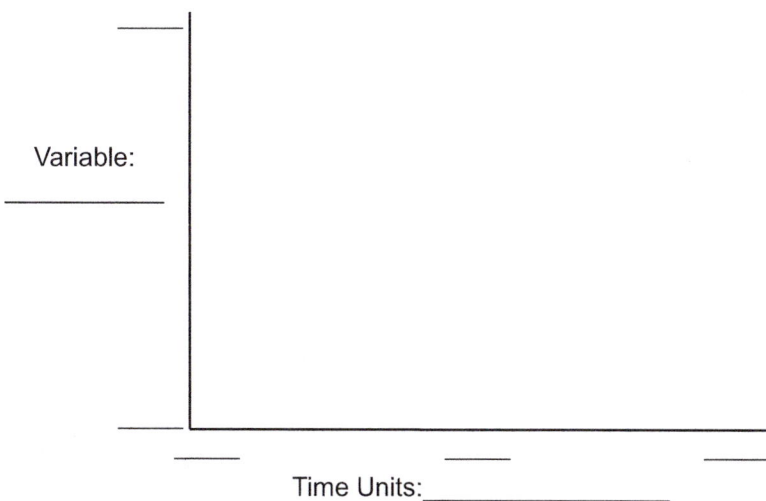

Graph Title:_____

Variable:
_____

Time Units:_____

Reflect
What did you change to create this result?

D Triple Dog Dare

1. Is there anything that would create a problem for the runner if he tries to speed up his training schedule? How could that be represented in the model?

Story 3: Learning to Rock
Overview

Eddie wants to join a rock band, but he doesn't know how to play the guitar. He decides to dedicate himself to learning to play the instrument. Use the model to help determine what skill to measure and to set a goal. A goal might be accuracy (e.g., percent notes played correctly) or speed (notes played per minute). Given the goal, how long will it take for his skill to be good enough to join a band?

Details

1. Time units_____
2. Playing ability (stock)_____
3. Playing goal_____
4. Time to learn_____

Guitar Frets, Tom Gally, Public Domain

D Dare

1. Re-label and change the numbers in the previous model to make sense for this situation.
2. Determine the best plan to achieve the goal.

D Double Dare

1. Using the model, think of at least two ways to increase how quickly Eddie can improve his skill.
2. Choose one idea and change the number for that part in the model to achieve the correct level more quickly. Make sure that your number is realistic. Sketch your best graph.

Graph Title:_____

_____

Variable:

_____

Time Units:_____

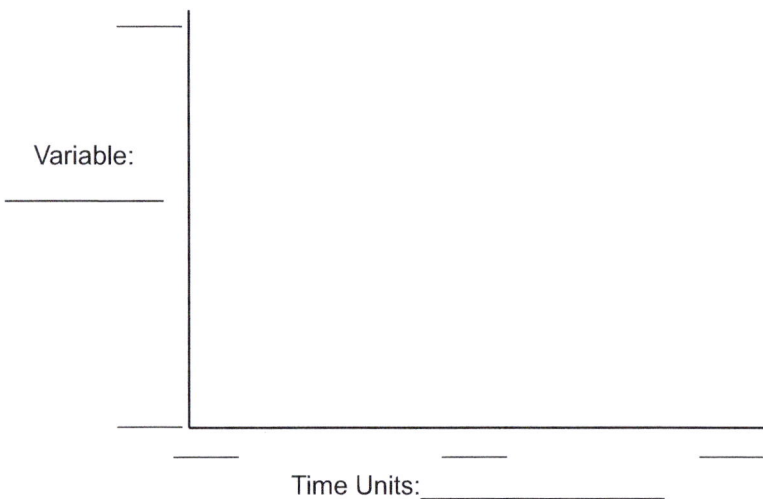

Reflect
What did you change to create this result?

D Triple Dog Dare

1. Change the model to show how Eddie could work on improving two different skills relating to playing the guitar. Consider how these two skills would impact his overall playing ability.

Story 4: Your Story

Create your own story with details, using an issue that behaves in a similar way. Modify the model to match your story, and use it to solve the problem(s).

Dare to Reflect:

One story I tried was_____

How did you adjust the model to solve the problem(s)? Create labels for the diagram and add any new part(s).

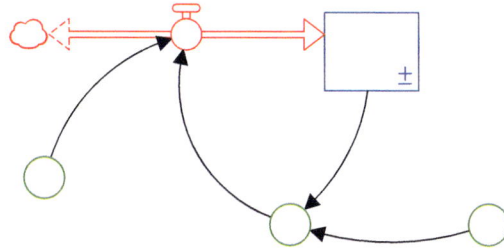

What would these model adjustments actually mean is happening in the real world?

Other thoughts and insights:

Chapter 4: Spreading Like Crazy

Social Media Tree, Public Domain

Dive in – How can you spread a new idea, like the desire to join a new social media site?

Ever wonder why some things spread and some things don't? Let's say that you have created your own new social media site and you want to get people to join. You start with one user and your goal is a million users.

How long would it take for use of the new site to spread? What would help the spread, so your new idea doesn't just die out?

🧩 Put Together the Pieces

First, you need some people. Create the following:

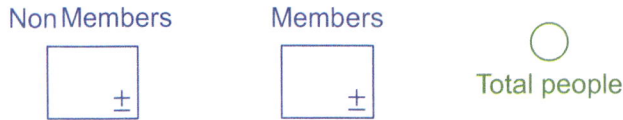

NonMembers   Members   Total people

The "NonMembers" can move to being "Members." Add a flow of "People joining."

NonMembers   People joining   Members

Now let's add the rest and connect all the parts as shown in the diagram below. The members can come in contact with "NonMembers," spreading the word about the new social media site.

The "Likelihood of spread" is based on how interesting the new site is to people who have heard of it. A 0.1 means that 10% of people who hear about it will join.

Each month, "Members" will talk with others about the site. These are "Contacts per member per month." A 10 indicates that this occurs ten times each month for each member. Some of these contacts will be between "Members" and "NonMembers."

Every month a new "NonMembers fraction" is calculated based on the "Total people" and how many "NonMembers" are left. It's important to keep in mind that "Total people" are not all the people in the world. You can think about these "Total people" as the people who would join your site if they were to come into frequent contact with other people who are current members.

Once you have all the parts connected, start adding the numbers and equations as indicated. See Appendix B: Equation Helper for assistance if needed.

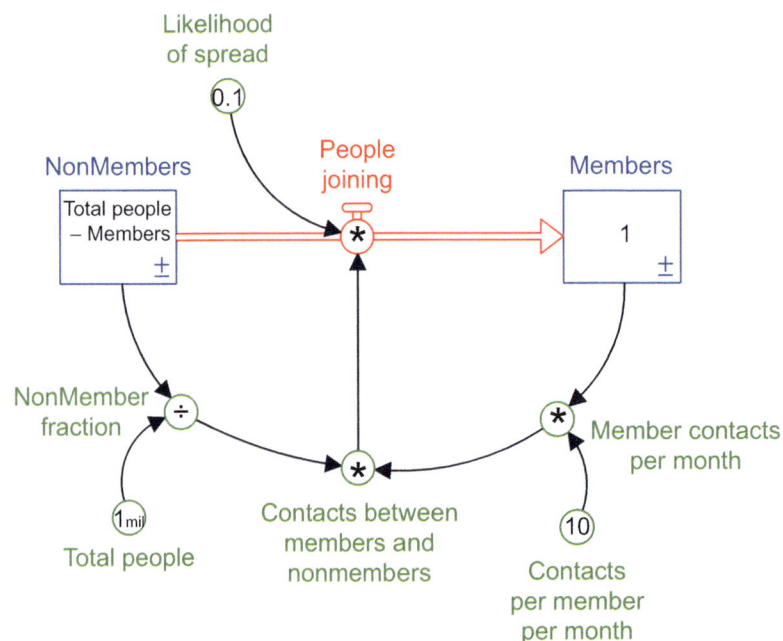

Set up the model's "Run Specs" as follows:
    Start Time = 0
    Stop Time = 12
    DT = 0.25 or 1/4
    Time Units = Months
    Integration Method = Euler

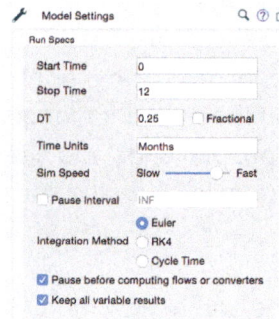

Also make sure that your stocks are set to allow negative values. In other words, if you are using Stella software, you must un-check the "Non-negative" box for each stock.

Create a graph with Members and NonMembers. You may need to set the graph's scale to match the one below.

Run the model to see what happens. If all the initial values are correctly entered, you should see the following graph lines and ending numerical values. If the behavior is different, recheck your connections and equations. If the behavior still does not match, check Appendix B: Equation Helper for guidance.

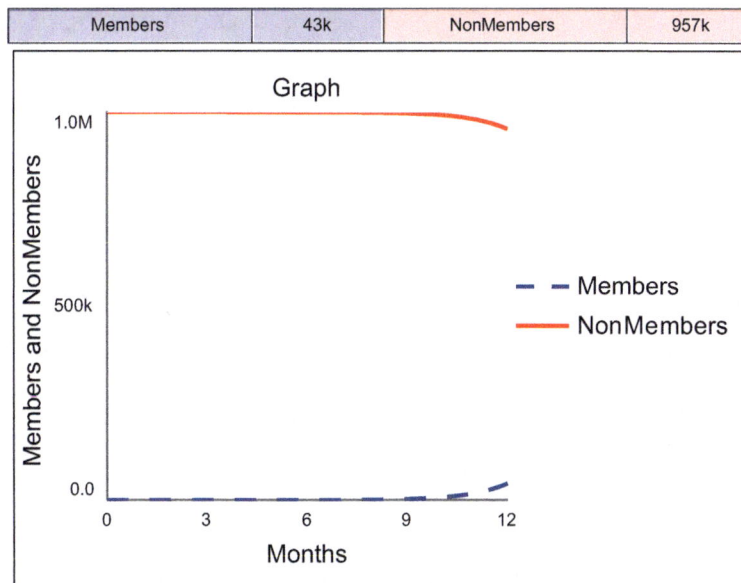

Members	43k	NonMembers	957k

🛠 Dare to Dig Deeper

Dare yourself to find solutions, using the model you created to help. Key questions to dig into are:
1. What happens if you run the model for longer than one year?
2. How can you get more people to join the site?
3. What happens if some people leave the site after awhile?

D Dare

1. Keeping the numbers the same, how many months will it take to have one million members? Hint: You'll need to change the number of months the model runs.
2. Sketch the graph and then check Appendix B: Equations Helper to see if your graph matches.

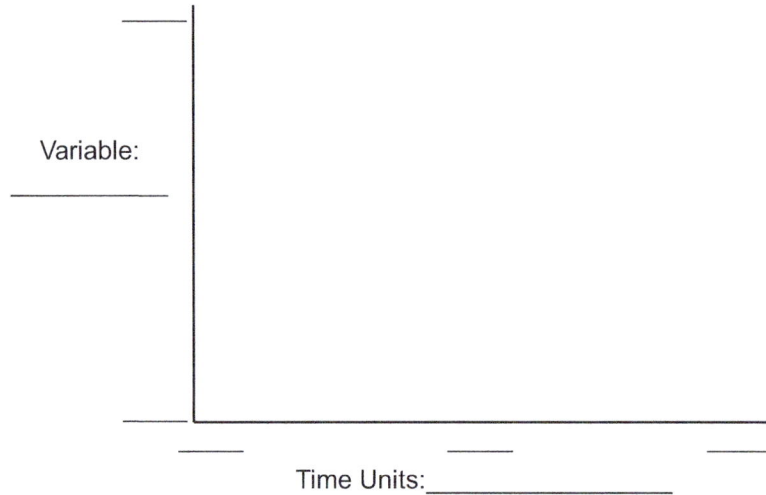

Graph Title:_____

Variable:
_____

Time Units:_____

D Double Dare

1. Using the model, think of at least three ways to speed up "NonMembers" joining the site.
2. Choose one idea and change the number for that part in the model to achieve faster growth. Make sure that your setting is realistic. For example, it's not reasonable for "Likelihood to spread" to be set to 1, indicating 100%.
3. Try some different ideas, and then sketch your best graph.

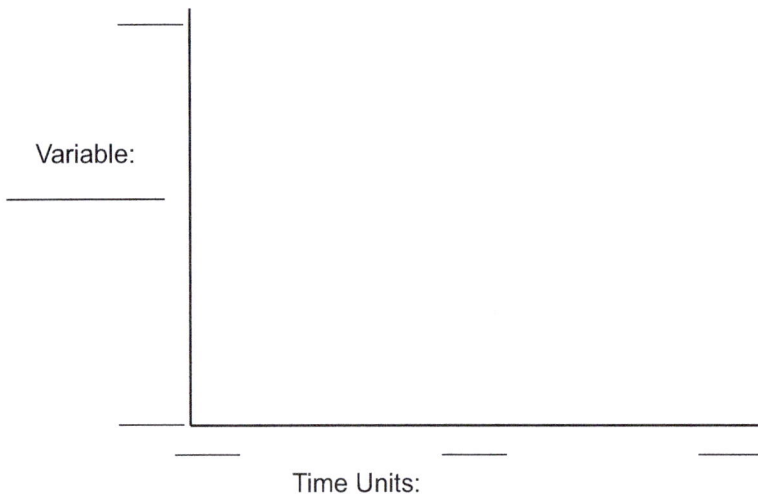

Graph Title:_____

Variable:
_____

Time Units:_____

Reflect
What did you change to create this result?

D Triple Dog Dare

1. Can you extend the model further to explore what would happen if, on average, "Members" leave the site after 10 months?
2. What could you do to minimize the number of members who leave?

Dare to Reflect:

What change(s) worked best to speed up "NonMembers" joining and prevent "Members" from leaving? Why? What would be happening in the real world if you could actually increase "People joining" or prevent "People leaving?" Show how you adjusted the model, adding any new parts.

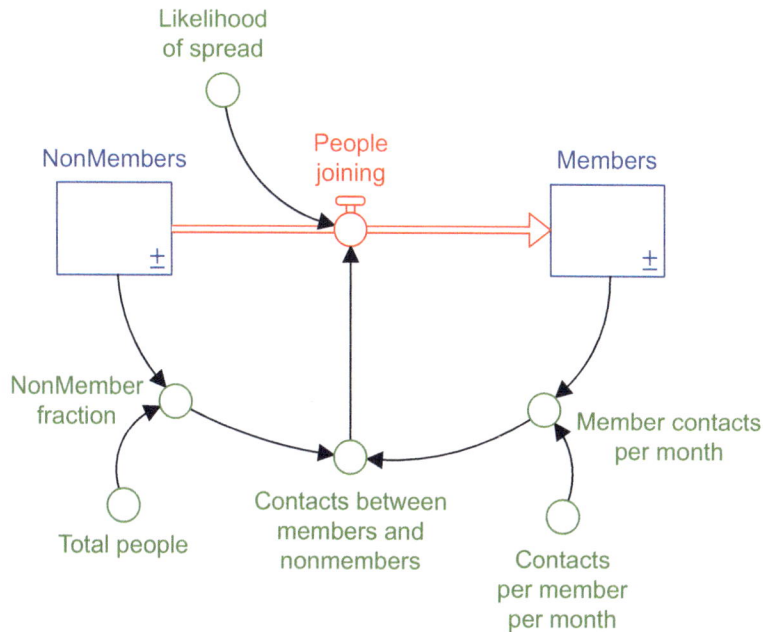

Likelihood
of spread

NonMembers   People   Members
                    joining

NonMember
fraction

Total people   Contacts between   Member contacts
                    members and   per month
                    nonmembers

                    Contacts
                    per member
                    per month

Thoughts and Insights from this Model:

Connect to Other Stories

Many other situations (real and fictional) behave in a similar way as this simple model does. Modify the labels and numbers for the social media model to explore one or more of these stories. You can even make up your own stories that have behaviors similar to those seen in this model.

Story 1: The Rumor Mill
Overview

A small group of students in a school know an unkind rumor about another student. They start sharing the rumor with other students, and it spreads throughout the school.

Details

1. Time units_____
2. Total students in the school_____
3. Students who don't know the rumor (stock)_____
4. Students who know rumor (stock)_____
5. Number of times each student shares the rumor per time unit_____
6. Percent chance that a new hearer will choose to spread the rumor_____

The Whisper, © Malcolm Campbell, Creative Commons 2.0, sculpture by Andre Wallace.

D Dare

1. Re-label and change the numbers in the previous model to make sense for this situation.
2. Determine how long it will take for the entire school to know the rumor. The lines on the graph should be similar to the social media "Dare" graph.

D Double Dare

1. Using the model, think of at least three ways to slow the spread of the rumor.
2. Choose one idea and change the number for that part in the model to achieve slower growth. Make sure that your number is realistic.
3. Try some different ideas and sketch your best graph.

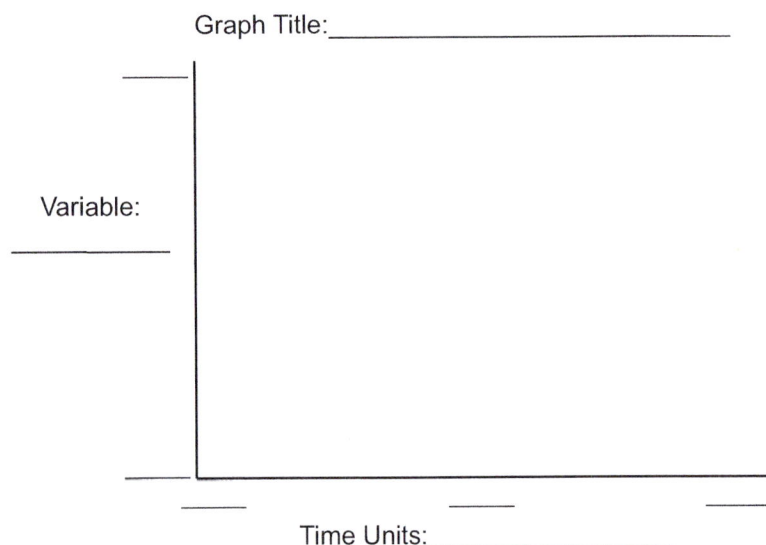

Graph Title:_____

Variable:

_____

Variable:
_____

Time Units:_____

Reflect
What did you change to create this result?

D Triple Dog Dare

1. Can you extend the model to explore what would happen if some of the people who have heard and started gossiping then choose to stop?
2. How can you decrease the number of people who are gossiping?

Story 2: Clan of Vampires Settling in New London
Overview

A family of vampires have settled in a large city called New London. They want to take over the entire city and make all the residents vampires (NOTE: They're not thinking about the long-term problems this could create for their own survival!)

Futuristic Architecture, Steve Maleny, Flickr Creative Commons 2.0

Details

1. Time units_____
2. Total population of New London_____
3. Non-vampires (stock)_____
4. Vampires (stock)_____
5. Bites per vampire per time unit_____
6. Percent chance of becoming a vampire when bitten_____

D Dare

1. Re-label and change the numbers in the previous model to make sense for this situation.
2. Determine how long it will take for the entire population of the city to become vampires. The lines on the graph should be similar to those in the social media graph.

D Double Dare

1. Using the model, think of at least three ways to slow the spread of new vampires.
2. Choose one idea and change the number for that part in the model to achieve slower growth. Make sure that your number is realistic.
3. Try some different ideas and sketch your best graph.

Graph Title:_____

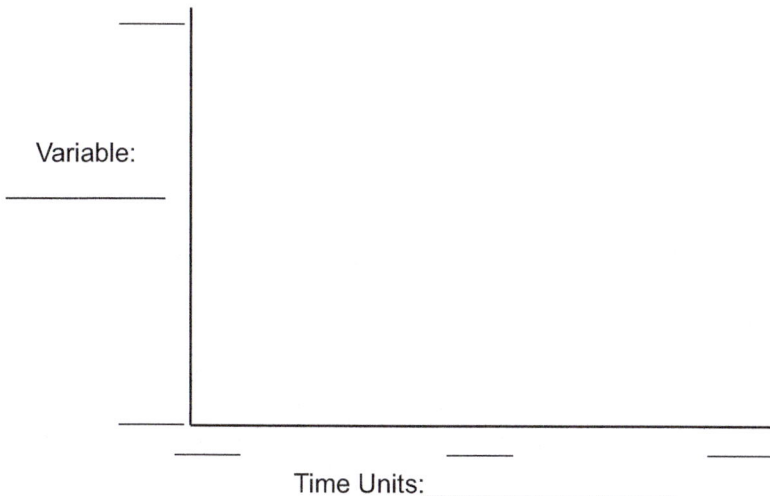

Variable:

_____

Time Units:_____

Reflect
What did you change to create this result?

D Triple Dog Dare

1. Can you extend the model to explore what would happen if some number of vampires decided that creating new vampires was a bad idea?
2. What could you do to decrease the number of vampires who bite people?

Story 3: Space Flu Spreading on Moonbase 22
Overview

A small group of people have a very serious form of space flu. Although no ones dies, once a person catches this flu, there's no cure.

Details

1. Time units_____
2. People on the moonbase_____
3. Healthy people (stock)_____
4. Sick people (stock)_____
5. Percent chance that flu spreads on contact_____
6. Contacts per day_____

Lunar Base, NASA, Public Domain

D Dare

1. Re-label and change the numbers in the previous model to make sense for this situation.
2. Determine how long it will take for the entire base to have space flu, assuming that no one visits other bases or recovers once they are sick. The lines on the graph should be similar to the social media graph.

D Double Dare

1. Using the model, think of at least three ways to slow down the spread of the flu.
2. Choose one idea and change the number for that part in the model to achieve slower growth. Make sure that your number is realistic.
3. Try some different ideas and sketch your best graph.

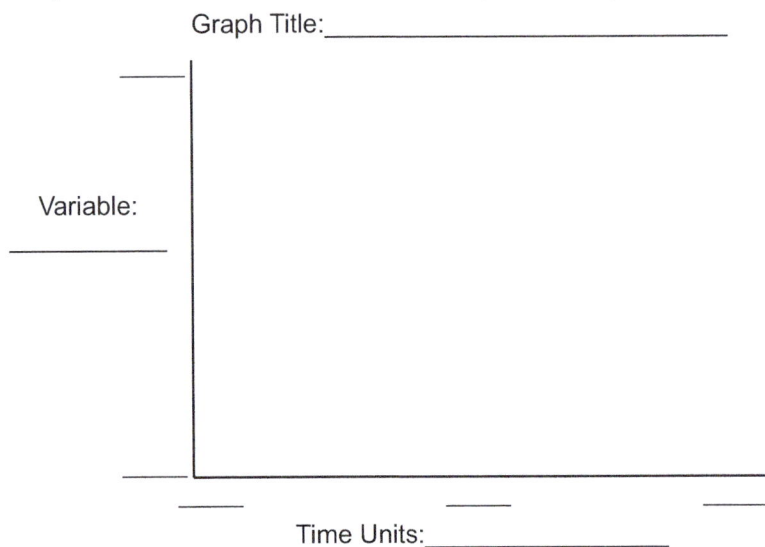

Graph Title:_____

Variable:
_____

Variable:
_____

Time Units:_____

Reflect
What did you change to create this result?

D Triple Dog Dare

1. Can you extend the model to explore what would happen if some of the people who have caught the flu eventually recover? Assume that they'll be immune from that strain of the flu if they recover. What could you do to maximize the number of people who recover?
2. Can you extend the model further to explore what would happen if some of the people died after getting the flu? What could you do to minimize the number of deaths?

Story 4: Your Story

Create your own story with details, using an issue that behaves in a similar way. Modify the model to match your story, and use it to solve the problem(s).

Dare to Reflect:

One story I tried was_____

How did you adjust the model to solve the problem(s)? Create labels for the diagram and add any new part(s).

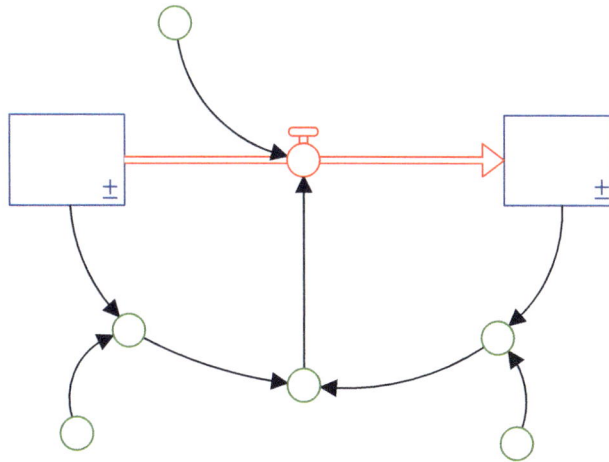

What would these model adjustments actually mean is happening in the real world?

Other thoughts and insights:

Chapter 5:
The Disappeared

The Twice Lost Tomb, "An All American Architecture," Public Domain

🐧 Dive in

Perhaps you've studied different peoples and cultures throughout history, and you may have noticed that some of them just disappeared. It's a mystery!

What caused those populations to grow? Why did they decline and, in some cases, disappear? One key aspect to consider is the role of resources: what resources did they need or desire, how did they use those resources, and did they face a scarcity of resources that led to their demise?

🧩 Put Together the Pieces

Part 1

First, you need some people and some resources they depend upon for survival. Create the following:

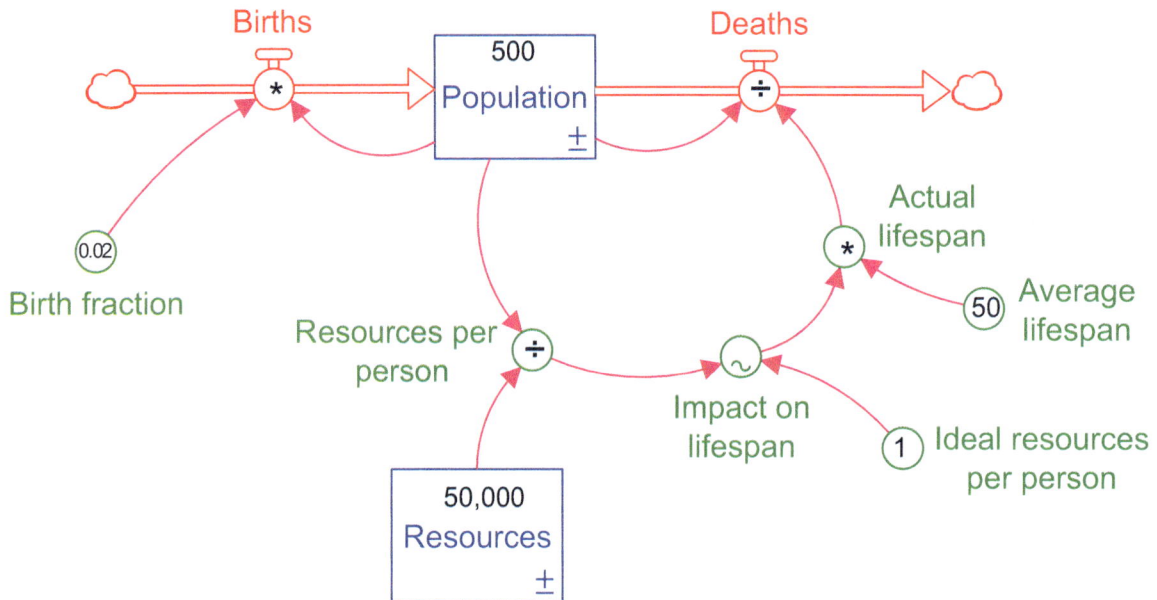

Input the numbers and equations as indicated in the diagram. See Appendix B: Equation Helper for assistance if needed. Note that "Impact on lifespan" has a tilde sign (~) and needs a special equation called a graphical function. A graphical function allows you to decide how the "Resources per person" affect the lifespan. If resources are scarce, then people will be more likely to die sooner than they would have otherwise. If resources are plentiful, then the lifespan will be the same as the "Average lifespan." Create the graphical function for "Impact on lifespan":

1. Input "Resources per person/Ideal resources needed per person" as the equation.
2. Click on the function 🖾 icon.
3. Check the box for "Graphical."
4. Set the y-axis scale to 0-1 for the "Impact on Lifespan" and the x-axis to 0-1.
5. Use the table to type in the values in order to create the line on the graph.

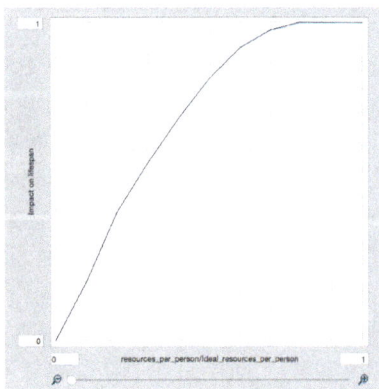

	x-axis - Res. per person/ Ideal res. per person	y-axis - Impact on lifespan (Output)
1	0	0
2	0.1	0.185
3	0.2	0.405
4	0.3	0.560
5	0.4	0.700
6	0.5	0.825
7	0.6	0.920
8	0.7	0.975
9	0.8	1
10	0.9	1
11	1	1

Also make sure that the stock is set to allow negative values. In other words, if you are using Stella software, you must un-check the "Non-negative" box for each stock you create.

Set up the model's "Run Specs" as follows:
    Start Time = 0
    Stop Time = 500
    DT = 0.125 or 1/8
    Time Units = Years
    Integration Method = RK4 (Runga Kutta 4)

Run the model, making sure that your model is producing a flat line (also called steady state) for the population. If not in steady state, recheck all your numbers and equations.

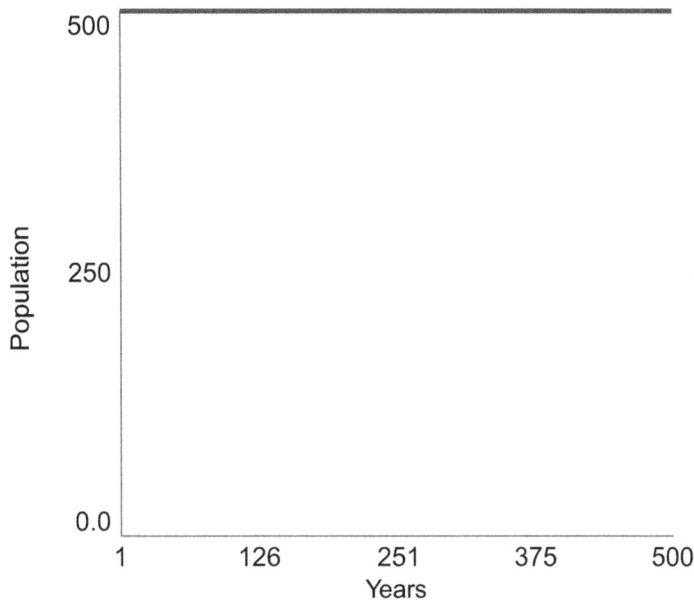

Experiment with changing the "Birth fraction," "Average lifespan," and "Ideal resources per person." Consider these questions as you explore:
1. What type of behaviors do you see?
2. What, if anything, causes the population to go down? Is the decline related to the amount of resources or something else?
3. What is missing in this model?

Part 2

At this point, none of the settings allow the "Population" to affect the amount of "Resources." In order for this to happen, an inflow and outflow for that stock are needed. Add to the structure as shown.

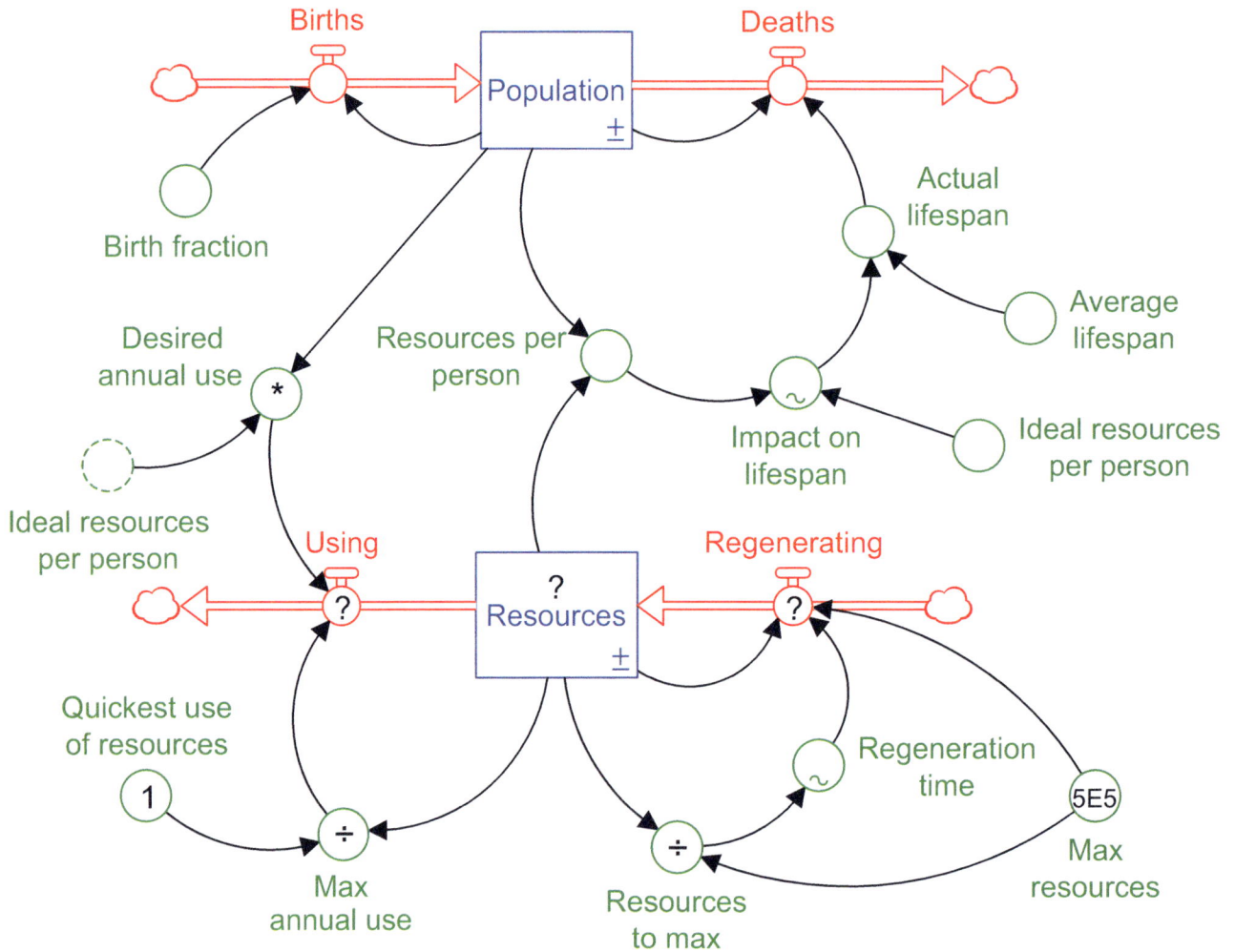

Add the new numbers and equations, noting the following:

1. "Ideal resources per person" is on the diagram twice. The second one (with the dotted lines) is called a "ghost" of the first, and it contains the same information as the original. If available, the "ghost" feature helps to prevent crossed lines, thus keeping your diagram clear and understandable.
2. "Max resources" is 5E5, which is a 5 with five zeros, or 50,000.
3. You need special equations for the stock and the two new flows as indicated here:

Part	Equation	What is this?
Resources	Max_resources*1	This means that the stock starts out a 100% of the possible resources. If the 1 is changed to a lower number, e.g., 0.5, that would indicate that there's a lot more space for resources to regenerate.
Regenerating	(Max_resources-Resources)/ Regeneration_time	The ability of the resource to grow is limited by some element, such as an amount of space. Having a maximum value makes the regeneration behavior more realistic.
Using	MIN(Desired_ annual_use, Max_ annual_use	If the resources run out, they can no longer be used. The model needs to check which is smaller – the resources individuals desire or the maximum amount of resources that are available.

Create another graphical function for the "Regeneration time." This function will set how long it takes for the resources to regenerate. If resources are plentiful, it takes less time to regenerate than if they're scarce.

1. Select "Resources to max" as the equation.
2. Click on the function ⊟ icon.
3. Check the box for "Graphical."
4. Set the y-axis scale to 1-100 for the "Regeneration time" and the x-axis to 0-1.
5. Use the table to type in the values in order to create the line on the graph.

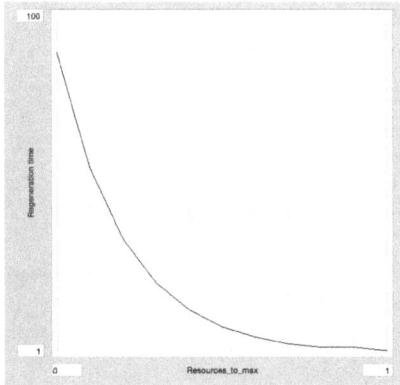

	y-axis - Resources_to_ max	x-axis - Regeneration time (Output)
1	0	89
2	0.1	55
3	0.2	34
4	0.3	21
5	0.4	13
6	0.5	8
7	0.6	5
8	0.7	3
9	0.8	2
10	0.9	1
11	1	1

Add Resources to your graph and run the model to make sure that it's still in steady state. This time, both "Population" and "Resources" should have flat lines. If you're using the free version of Stella online, both of these graphs must be on the same graph pad. They are shown separately here to make the very different scales more clear.

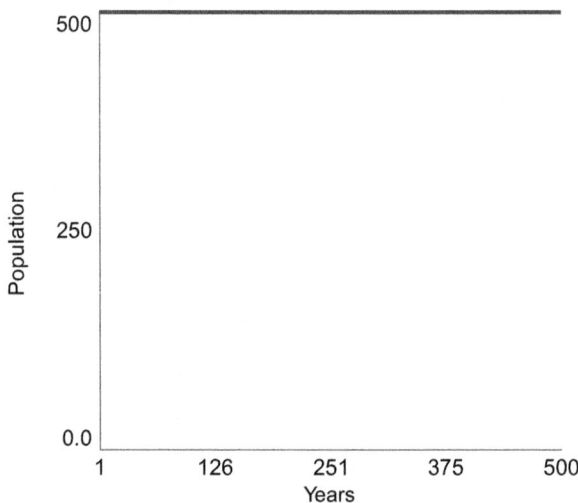

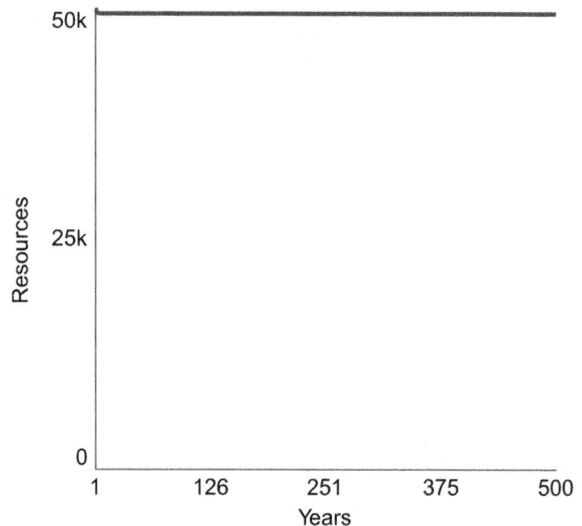

Dare to Dig Deeper

So far, there's no problem. The population and resources are stable. In many societies, historically and right now, this is not the case. Populations often grow, sometimes very rapidly, depleting their resources along the way. Even if a population is not growing, people may wish to use more and more resources.

D Dare

1. Change the "Average lifespan" to 75 years, rather than 50, and run the model again. What happens to the population and resources?
2. Sketch your most interesting graphs for population and resources. You can plot them both on the same graph, or create a second graph on another page.

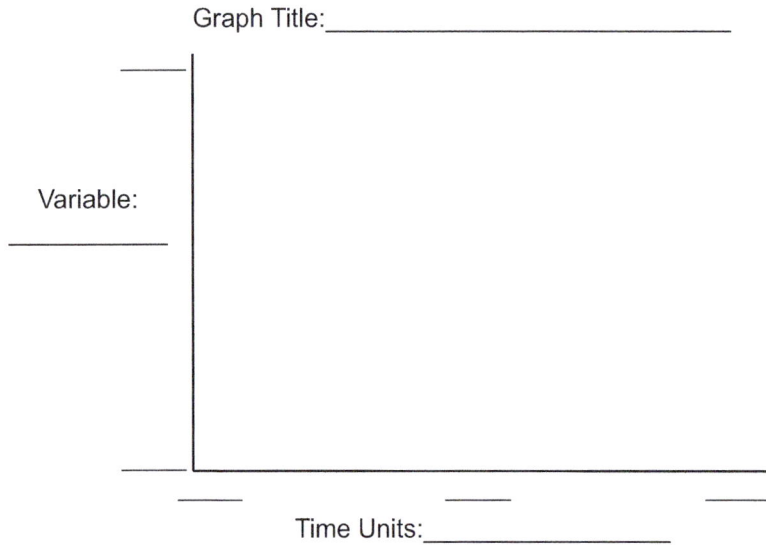

Graph Title:_____

Variable:
_____

Time Units:_____

D Double Dare

1. Explore how the model behaves if you change the resources or what affects them. For example, what if each individual wants more or fewer resources per individual? What if you start with half as many resources? (Equation for this is Max_resources*0.5)
2. Try some different ideas, and then sketch your most interesting graphs.

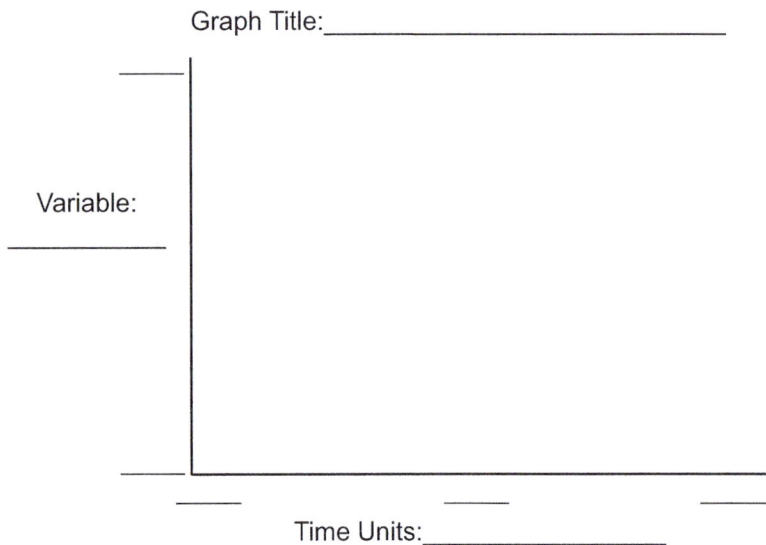

Graph Title:_____

Variable:
_____

Time Units:_____

Reflect
What did you change to create this result?

D

Triple Dog Dare

1. Experiment with the model by trying as many different changes as you can, making sure that they are realistic. Also consider adding parts to the model to create different results. Is there any way to prevent the population from crashing?

Dare to Reflect:

Think about how this model might apply in real-world or fictional situations and also what its limitations might be.

Thoughts and Insights from this Model:

Connect to Other Stories

Many other situations (real and fictional) behave in a similar way as this model does. Modify the labels and numbers for the population/resource model to explore one or more of these stories. You can even make up your own stories that have behaviors similar to those seen in this model.

Story 1: Easter Island
Overview

Easter Island is a well-known case of a population that came close to dying out. Although many factors were involved in the final crash, such as slave-traders who kidnapped the islanders, one big part of the problem arose because the islanders cut down the trees faster than they could regenerate. The trees were a key resource needed for success. For example, they built boats from the wood to fish, an important aspect of their diet.

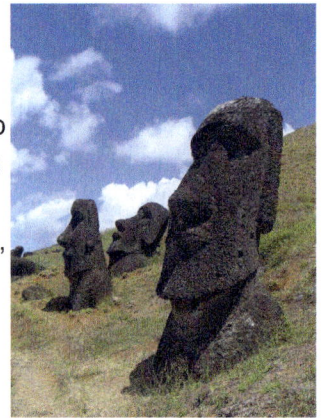

Spend a little time exploring theories about Easter Island in order to apply the model to the islanders' situation. Many sites exist online that describe what likely happened there[7].

Moai, A. Urbina, Public Domain

D Dare

1. Re-label and change the numbers in the previous model to make sense for this situation. Make sure to show a scenario in which the population is initially rising and the trees decline as a result.
2. Determine how similar/different the model behavior is to what actually happened on Easter Island.

D Double Dare

1. Using the model, think of at least two ways that would have prevented the population and resource from collapsing.
2. Choose one idea and change the number for that part in the model to change the outcome. Make sure that your number is realistic. Sketch your best graphs.

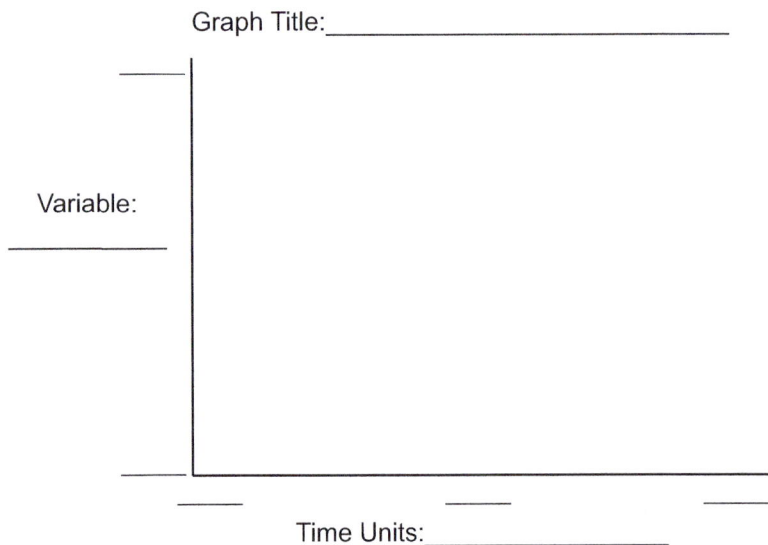

Graph Title:_____

Variable:
_____

Time Units:_____

Reflect
What did you change to create this result?

D Triple Dog Dare

1. Can you add something to the model to show how the islanders might have handled the use of resources in a way that prevents the crash?
2. What other peoples in history have experienced a similar pattern of collapse?

---

7   For example, http://www.pbs.org/wgbh/nova/ancient/pioneers-of-easter-island.html

Story 2: Mayan Society
Overview

The Maya lived in Central America. They built great cities that had population densities simlar to modern-day Los Angeles, CA. For 1200 years, they dominated the area, but in the end their society collapsed, like so many others before and after. They deforested and destroyed the very landscape that supported them. As the trees disappeared, drought became worse, which made it difficult to provide enough food and water to the population.

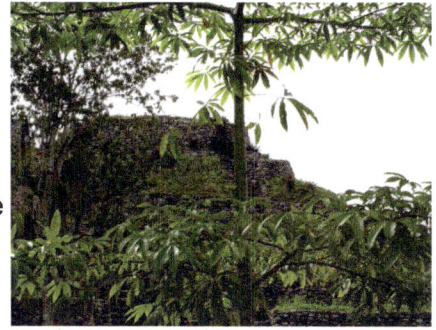

Temple, C.T. Liotta, Public Domain

Spend a little time researching the Maya in order to apply the model to their situation. Many sites exist online that describe what likely happened there, based on many different research studies.

D Dare

1. Re-label and change the numbers in the previous model to make sense for this situation. Make sure to show a scenario in which the population is initially rising and the trees decline as a result.
2. Determine how similar/different the model behavior is to what actually happened to Mayan society.

D Double Dare

1. Using the model, think of at least two ways that would have prevented the population crash.
2. Choose one idea and change the number for that part in the model to change the outcome. Make sure that your number is realistic. Sketch your best graph.

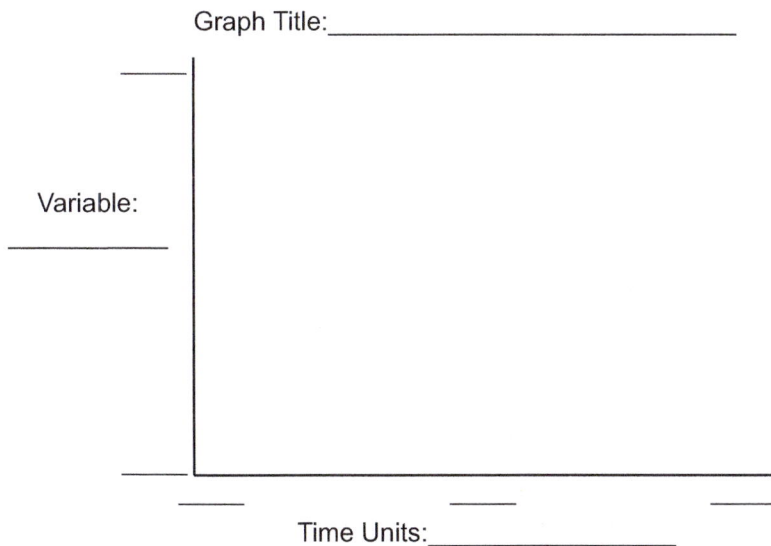

Graph Title:_____

Variable:
_____

Time Units:_____

Reflect
What did you change to create this result?

D Triple Dog Dare

1. Can you add something to the model to show how the Maya might have handled the use of resources in a way that prevents the crash?
2. What other peoples in history have experienced a similar pattern of collapse?

Story 3: Our World
Overview

If you look at the data for population growth in our world, the numbers are still growing exponentially (in other words, really, really fast). What could the stock of resources represent? In other words, what is required for survival of any species?

Earth from Apollo 17, NASA, Public Domain

D Dare

1. Change the numbers in the previous model to make sense for this situation. Make sure to show a scenario in which the global population is growing.
2. Determine how long it takes for resources to decline.
3. How does the model connect to real-world situations related to populations and resources?

D Double Dare

1. Using the model, think of at least two ways to prevent a decline of resources and a subsequent population crash.
2. Choose one or more ideas to prevent a resource and population decline. Make sure that your numbers are realistic. Sketch your best graph.

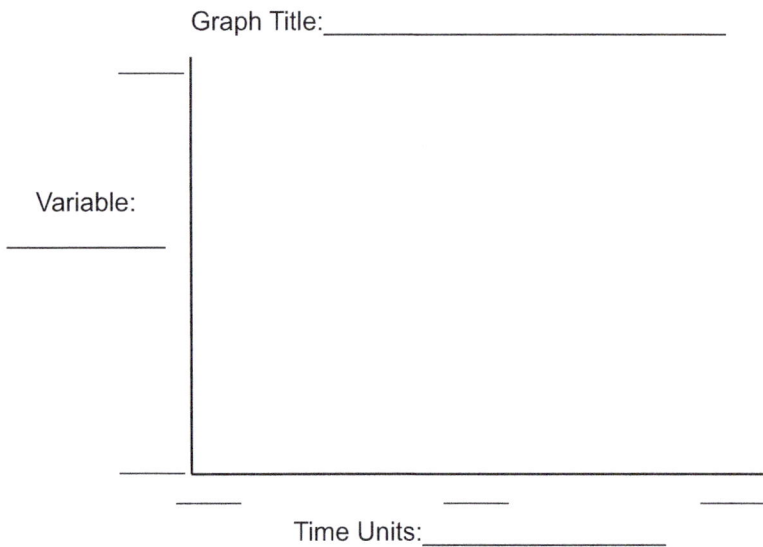

Graph Title:_____

Variable:
_____

Variable:
_____

Time Units:_____

Reflect
What did you change to create this result?

D Triple Dog Dare

1. Can you add elements to the model to show...
    - how societies today handle a population that's growing too quickly or too slowly?
    - how decisions by individual countries affect the world as a whole?

Story 4: Your Story

Create your own story with details, using an issue that behaves in a similar way. Modify the model to match your story, and use it to solve the problem(s).

Dare to Reflect:

One story I tried was_____

How did you adjust the model to solve the problem(s)? Create labels for the diagram and add any new part(s).

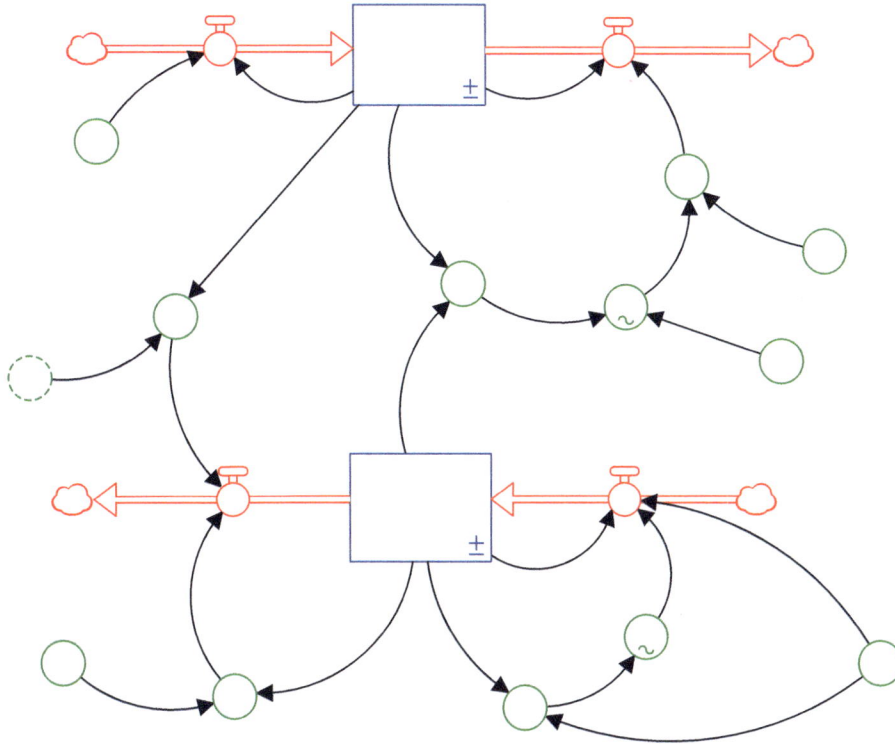

What would these model adjustments actually mean is happening in the real world?

Other thoughts and insights:

Chapter 6:
Stuck in a Rut

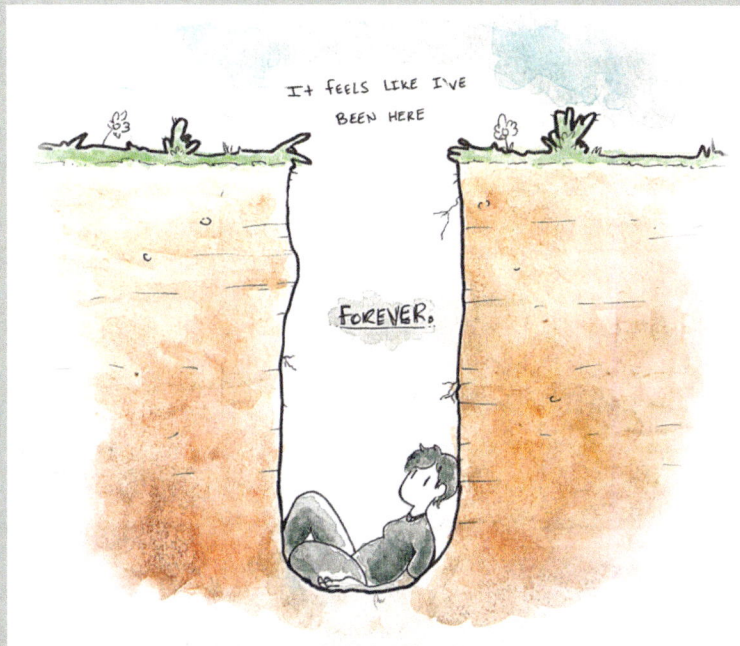

Stuck in a Rut, ©Charpener on Deviant Art, Used with permission

🤿 Dive in

Have you ever heard the phrase "I'm stuck in a rut?" Perhaps you want to do something different, but you keep on doing the same old thing anyway. Often this behavior is grounded in deeply ingrained habits. Think of these as patterns of thinking and behaving that are so strongly part of your life that it's hard to let go of them.

The challenge here is to understand why it's so hard to change a habit and to think about how to change habits not just in the short term, but in the long term.

🧩 Put Together the Pieces

Create the two stocks shown below, keeping in mind that they are slightly different in their meaning. The "Habit" stock shows how much you actually DO a particular behavior as a percent. We assume at the beginning, that habit is engaged in 100% of the time. The "Deeply ingrained habit" shows to what degree this habit is embedded in your very way of thinking and acting. It's also a percent, so at the beginning, this habit is very strong, at 100%. These two stocks affect one another, so the more ingrained the habit is, the more likely your behavior will show that. At the same time, the more you engage in the habit, the more ingrained it becomes.

Note that both of the inflows can run in both directions, as biflows, so make sure to create the correct type of flow. Also make sure that the stock is set to allow negative values. In other words, if you are using Stella software, you must un-check the "Non-negative" box for each stock you create.

Input the numbers as indicated. Notice that no equations are indicated for the flows. See if you can figure out what calculations are needed for the flows. Keep in mind that the stocks should not go over 100 or under 0, since they're based on percents.

Hints:
- You'll only need some combination of subtraction, multiplication and division in the flows.
- Order of operations matters, so insert parentheses when needed.
- See Appendix B: Equation Helper for assistance if needed.

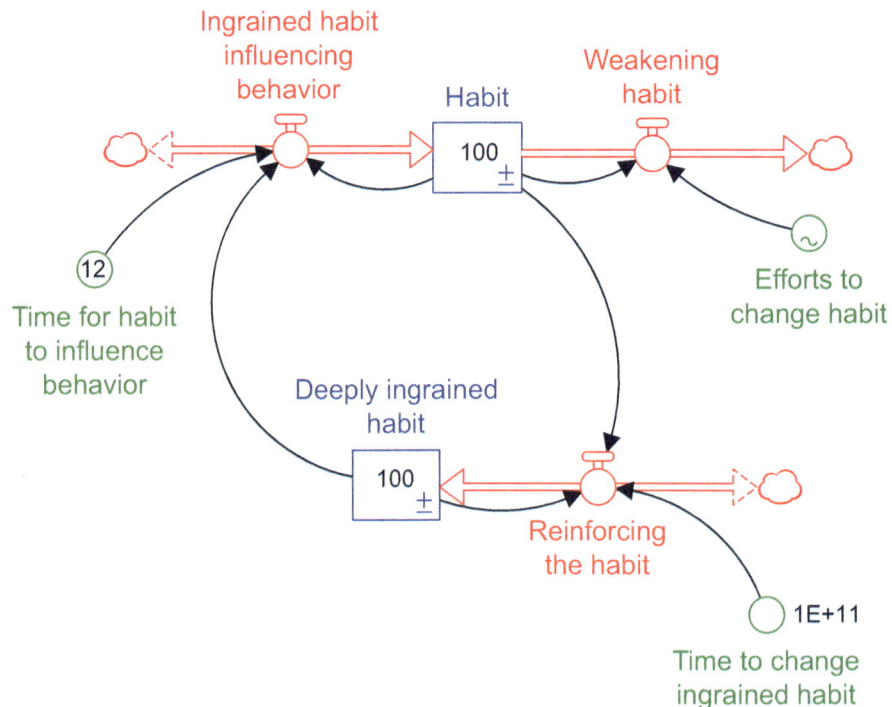

Notice a few details about this model. "Time to change ingrained habit" is 1E+11, which is a "1" with 11 zeros after it. That's equal to 1 billion months. "Time for habit to influence behavior" is set to 12 to indicate that it takes an average of 12 months for a "Deeply ingrained habit" to become established.
The tilde on "Efforts to change habit" means we'll need a graphical function.

Type "TIME" as the output equation for "Efforts to change habit." The graph shows how much effort is put into reducing the habit for months 0 to 60. Set the graph to zero (0) effort all the way across the timeline.

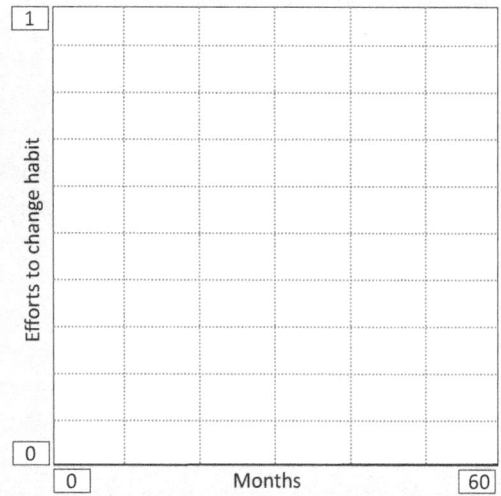

Set up the model's "Run Specs" as follows:
Start Time = 0
Stop Time = 60
DT = 0.125 or 1/8
Time Units = Months
Integration Method = Euler

Run the model, making sure it is producing a flat line (also called steady state) for the "Habit" and the "Deeply ingrained habit." If not in steady state, recheck all your numbers and equations.

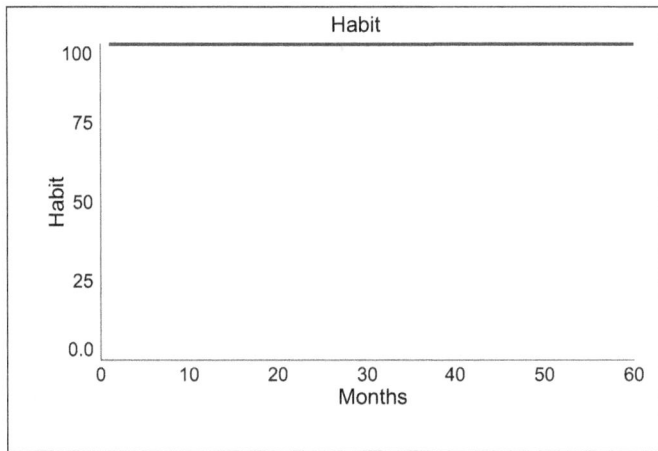

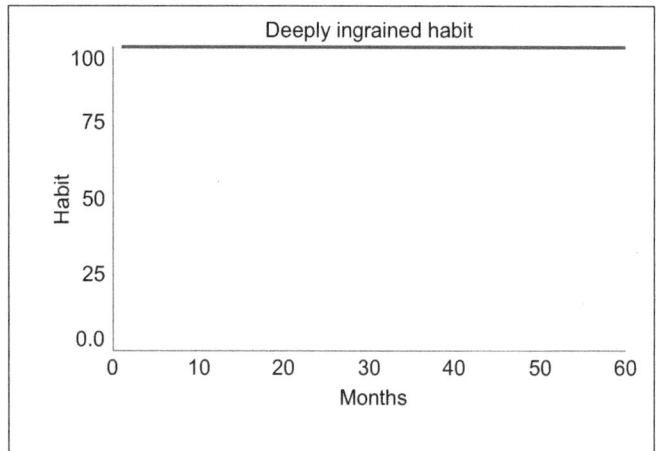

Change the graphical function as shown here. This graph shows how much effort is being put into stopping a particular habit. For months 0-10, no effort is put forth. For months 20 to 30, the effort ramps up to 0.5 (or halfway), staying at that level for 10 months. Then the effort ramps back down again, until there's no effort for months 40 to 60.

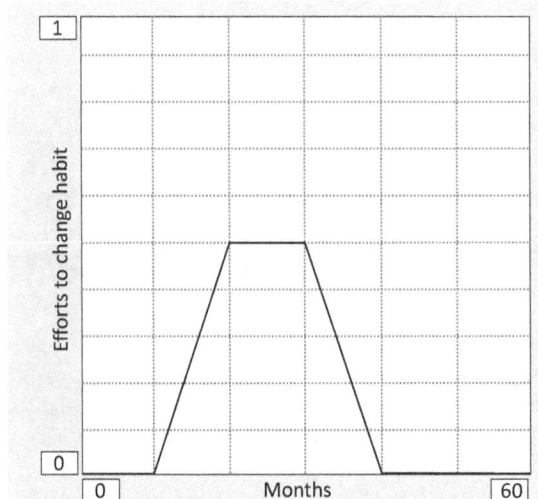

Run the model again and confirm that it is producing the behavior shown. If not, recheck all your numbers and equations in Appendix B: Equation Helper.

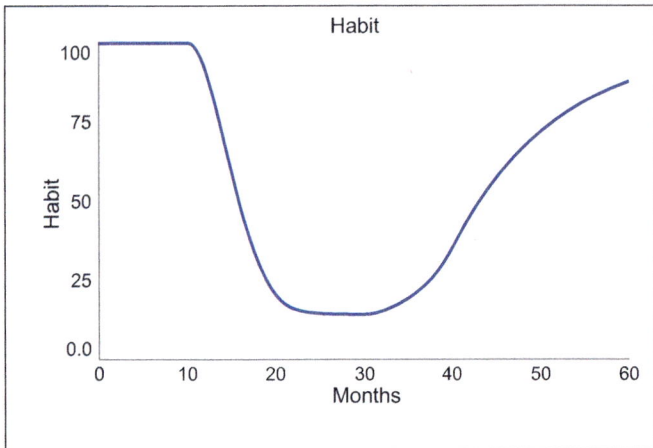

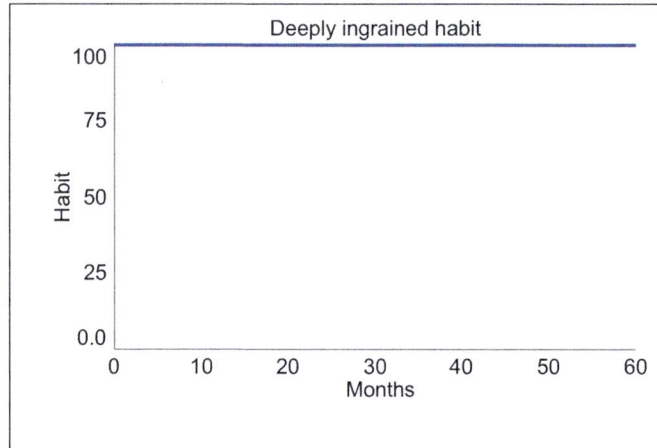

Notice what's happening to the "Habit." As soon as the effort increases at month 10, the "Habit" behavior goes down. As soon as the effort decreases, starting at month 30, the "Habit" behavior goes right back up again. The "Deeply ingrained habit" doesn't change at all.

That's a big problem. Despite a lot of effort for more than two years, the habit just returns almost to its original level. How disappointing! One important reason for this is that the "Deeply ingrained habit" doesn't go down at all. That's because the "Time to change..." is so large (100 billion months), indicating that it's a habit that's essentially impossible to change.

Change the "Time to change ingrained habit" to 36 months, removing the 1E+11 equation. How does this change the pattern of behavior for the "Habit?" Now try 10 months. You should see the set of graphs below, showing the three different scenarios/runs.

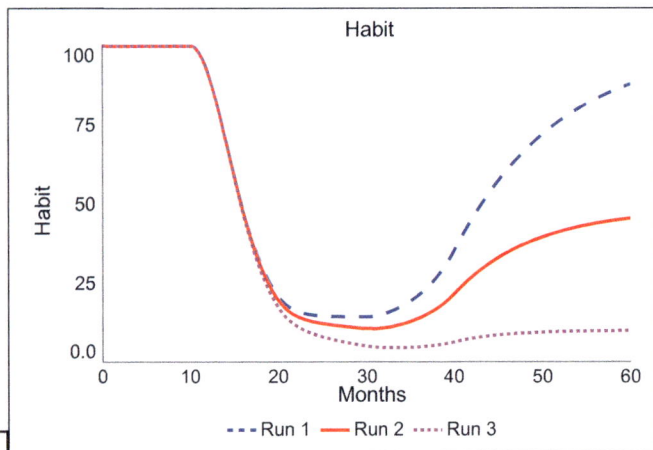

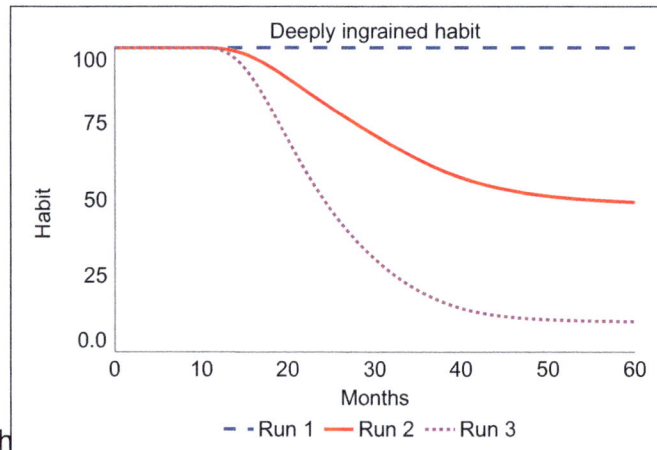

in the red (middle, solid) line? Which habits could you change quickly, as in the pink (bottom, dotted) line? Which ones are almost impossible to change, as in the blue (top, dashed) line?

being sedentary	procrastinating (studies)	forgetting to brush your teeth
smoking	staying up late	drinking coffee
watching TV	biting fingernails	forgetting your lunch
wearing a hat	other?	

Dare to Dig Deeper

Let's look at some real habits and how they could change over time.

D Dare

1. Think of a specific habit you'd like to change. Set the "Time to change ingrained habit" to make sense for this situation. Sketch the graph showing your effort in the past.
2. Try changing the "Efforts to change habit" graph to explore whether you can reduce the habit in the future. Sketch your most interesting set of habit graphs. You can plot them both on the same graph or create a second graph on another page.

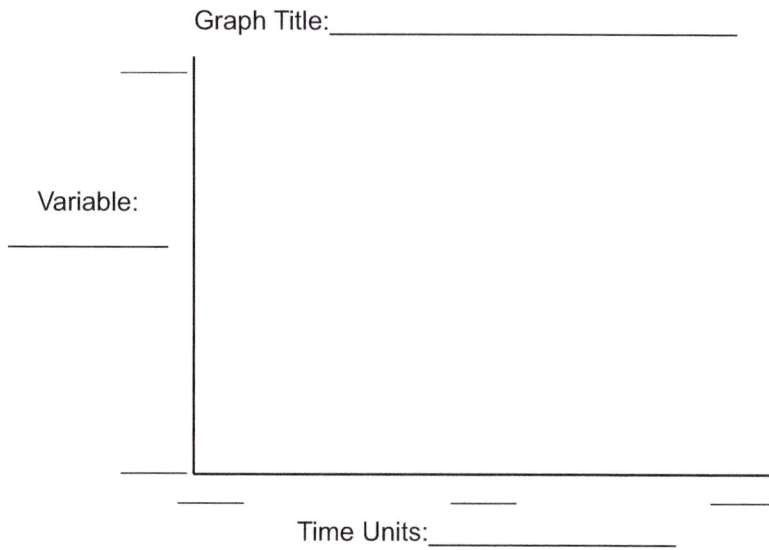

Graph Title:_____

Variable:
_____

Time Units:_____

D Double Dare

1. Explore how the model behaves if you change how strong a habit is to start by setting one or both of the stock values to something lower than 100. How is the behavior similar/different?
2. Try some different ideas, and then sketch your most interesting graphs.

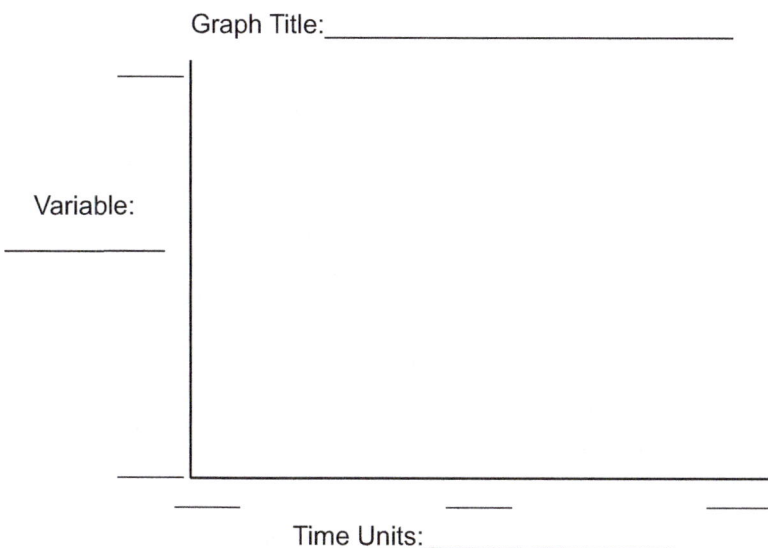

Graph Title:_____

Variable:
_____

Time Units:_____

Reflect
What did you change to create this result?

D
Triple Dog Dare

1. What is the best way to eliminate an undesirable habit? Try changing different elements, continuing to think about a habit in your own life.

Dare to Reflect:

Think about how this model might apply in real-world or fictional situations and also what its limitations might be.

Thoughts and Insights from this Model:

Connect to Other Stories

Many other situations (real and fictional) behave in a similar way as this model does. Modify the labels and numbers for the habits model to explore one or more of these stories. You can even make up your own stories that have behaviors similar to those seen in this model.

Story 1: Product Loyalty
Overview

Companies that have a product to sell want you to buy that product, not just once, but over and over. To do that, they must influence your beliefs about the product and also your routines for using that product. Imagine also that initially, you do not have a habit of purchasing that product. Maybe you've tried it a few times, but you haven't purchased it exclusively.

Shopping for Groceries, NARA, Public Domain

D Dare

1. Re-label and change the numbers in the previous model to make sense for this situation. Add some parts to the model to show how you can strengthen (add to) a habit. You'll need to make sure that the habit can't go over 100%. You'll also need to start the habit stocks at low numbers to begin.
2. Make sure to show a scenario in which buying a particular product tends to become ingrained over time.

D Double Dare

1. Using the model, think of at least two ways to help the company gain a customer's loyalty.
2. Choose one idea and change the number for that part in the model to increase the habit. Make sure that your number is realistic. Sketch your best graphs.

Graph Title:_____

Variable:

Time Units:_____

Reflect
What did you change to create this result?

D Triple Dog Dare

1. Can you add something to the model to show how a company can prevent the loss of a customer?
2. What other situations are similar to this one?

Story 2: Strengthening a Habit
Overview
What if you wanted to strengthen a habit instead of eliminate it? How could you modify and use this model to consider that question?

Runner, U.S. Air Force, Public Domain

D Dare

1. Re-label and change the numbers in the previous model to make sense for this situation. Add some parts to the model to show how you can strengthen (add to) a habit. You'll need to make sure that the habit can't go over 100%. You'll also need to start the habit stocks at low numbers to begin.
2. Make sure to show a scenario in which practicing a particular habit tends to become ingrained over time.

D Double Dare

1. Using the model, think of at least two ways to strengthen a habit.
2. Choose one idea and change the number for that part in the model to establish a new habit. Sketch your best graph.

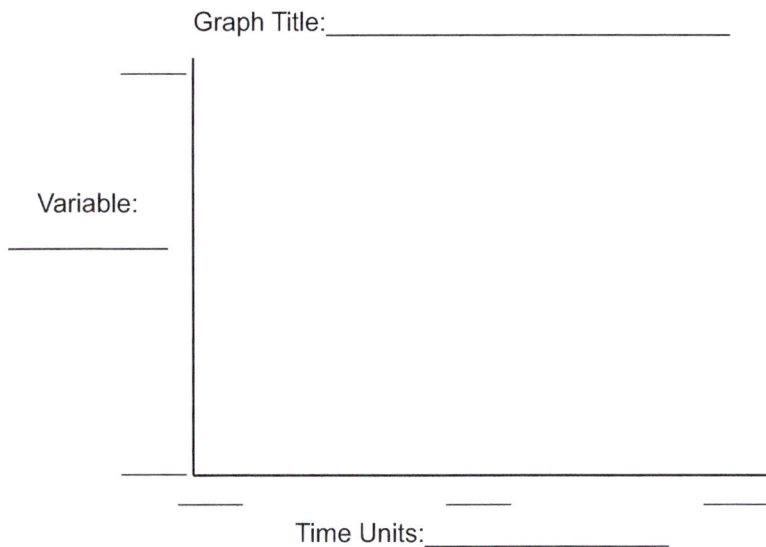

Graph Title:_____

_____

Variable:
_____

Time Units:_____

Reflect
What did you change to create this result?

D Triple Dog Dare

1. Can you add something to the model to show how forces also attempt to weaken a new good habit at the same time you're trying to strengthen it?
2. What other situations are similar to this one?

Story 3: Your Story

Create your own story with details, using an issue that behaves in a similar way. Modify the model to match your story and use it to improve a situation.

Dare to Reflect:

One story I tried was_____

How did you adjust the model to improve a situation? Create labels for the diagram and add any new part(s).

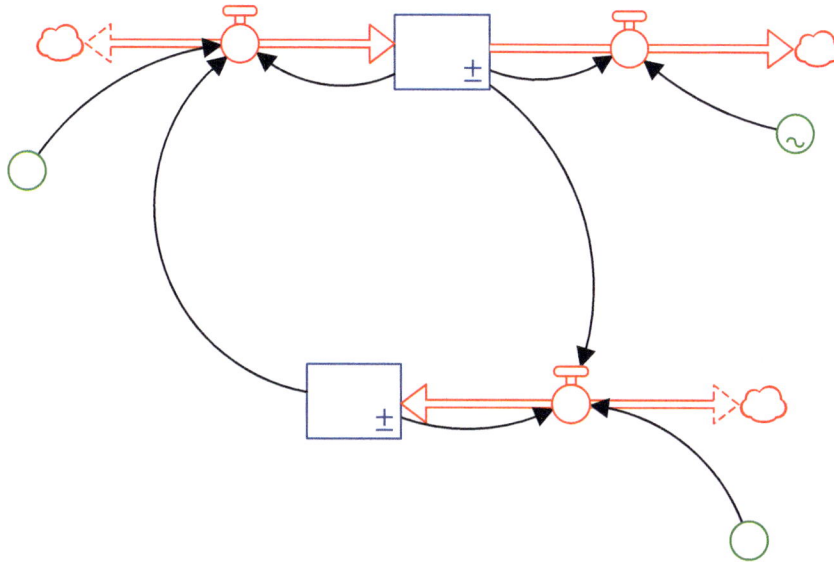

What would these model adjustments actually mean is happening in the real world?

Other thoughts and insights:

Man changing light statue in Lodz, Guillaume Speurt, Creative Commmons 2.0

🤿 Dive in

This chapter is a little different from the first six. Rather than just building and modifying a model to explore an issue, here you can work to fix a model that's broken or not behaving in a logical manner. Fixing models is one way to get better at modeling systems.

A model's structure and equations affect how it behaves. Adjustments can change what happens over time. As in previous chapters, each model has a story that the model represents. Your challenge is to change the models in a way that fixes the issues and creates behaviors that make sense.

Challenge 1: The Hatfields and the McCoys

Consider the Story

Gun violence, of course, is not a topic to make light of. This story can generate discussion around this challenging topic by creating (or in this case, fixing) a simple model. Using an example like this from history can be an helpful way to talk about gun violence prevention. Here's the story: back in the 1800s, a famous feud arose between two families in West Virginia and Kentucky – the Hatfields and the McCoys. As the story goes, violence arose between the two families for a number of reasons. For example, one family member was killed over a question of who owned a particular hog. The violence continued, with one killing leading to the next, often for reasons of revenge.

So, the basic dynamic of this loop is that the more McCoys there are, the more Hatfields are shot by McCoys, so there are fewer Hatfields. The fewer Hatfields shoot fewer McCoys, so there are more McCoys. The more McCoys, the more they shoot Hatfields, and so on. Of course this story makes no sense at all, because killing can't lead to a greater number of people. It can only lead to fewer people.

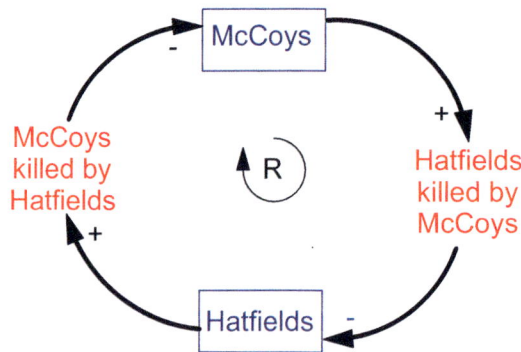

Build the Model

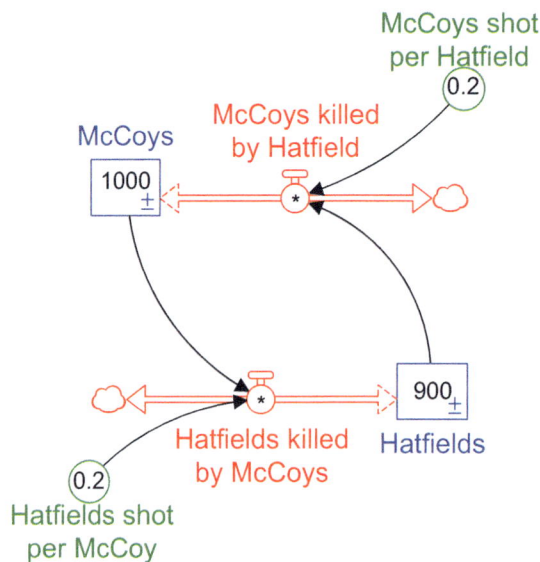

Build the model below and input the numbers and equations as indicated in the diagram. See Appendix B: Equation Helper for assistance if needed. Note that both flows are outflows (to show numbers killed) that have the biflow option selected. As always, don't forget to uncheck the "Non-negative" box.

Set up the model's "Run Specs" as follows:

> Start Time = 0
> Stop Time = 12
> DT = 0.25 or 1/4
> Time Units = Months
> Integration Method = Euler

Run the model and see what happens. You should get the graph shown here.

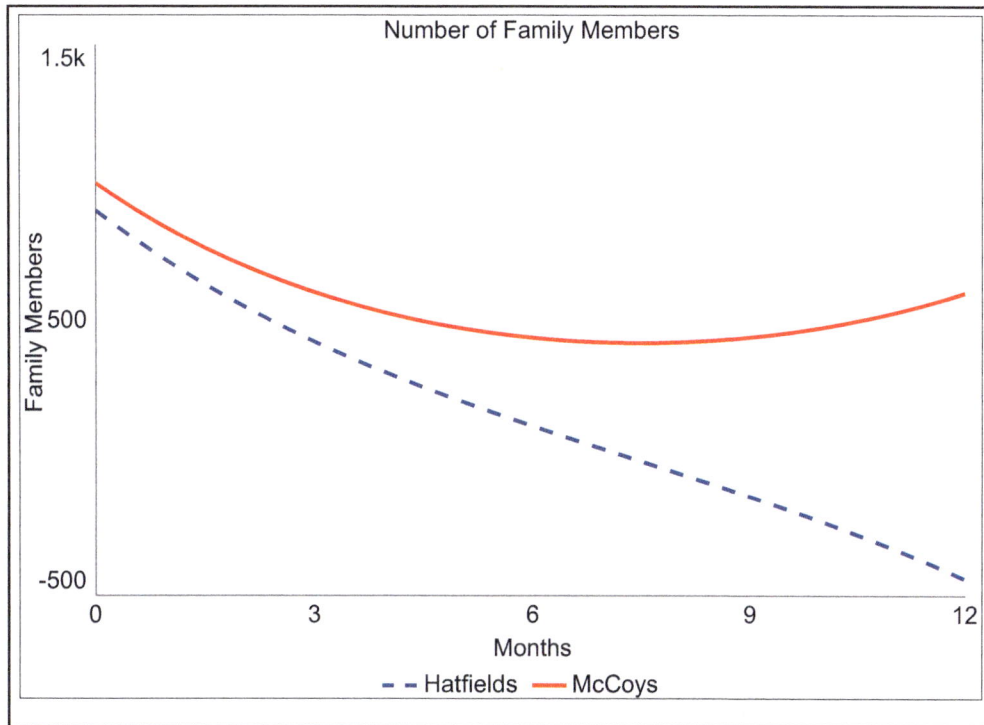

Problem:

What is the problem with the model behavior? Think about whether the graphs for Hatfields and McCoys make sense.
What on the graph is impossible?

Hatfield Clan, Public Domain

Fix the Model

How can you prevent the "Hatfields" from becoming negative? In the real world, we obviously can't have a negative number of people. The other problem is that the "McCoys" go up near the end. That's not possible either, since the flow is "McCoys killed...."

Using your skills gained using graphical functions (Chapters 2 and 5), how can you change the model in order to prevent this problem? Keep in mind:

1. Do not select the "Non-negative" box for the stocks. This would be a Band-Aid approach, but it does not fix the underlying problem.
2. The "Hatfields shot per McCoy" *depends* on the stock of "Hatfields." In fact, the number shot must be zero when the number of Hatfields is zero. The "McCoys shot per Hatfield" also *depends* on the stock of "McCoys."(That means you'll need two more arrows in your diagram to show those dependencies.)
3. Eventually the "Hatfields" totally die out, and the "McCoys" decrease as shown.

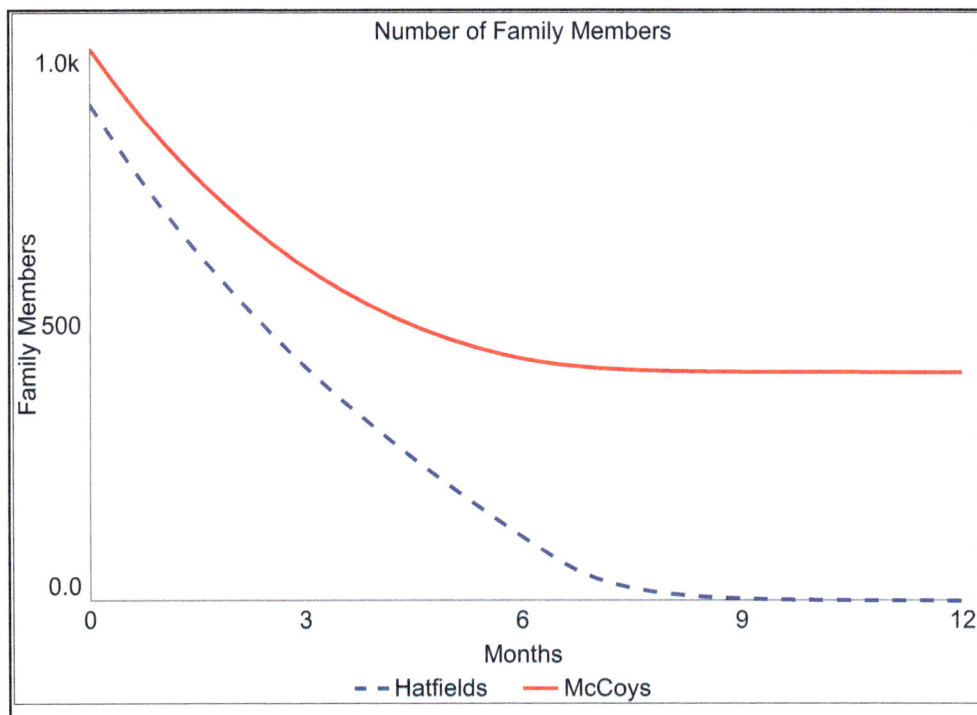

If you get stuck, you can check the example model online or the hints in Appendix B.

Reflection

How did you fix the model to create results that make sense? Indicate what you did on the diagram.

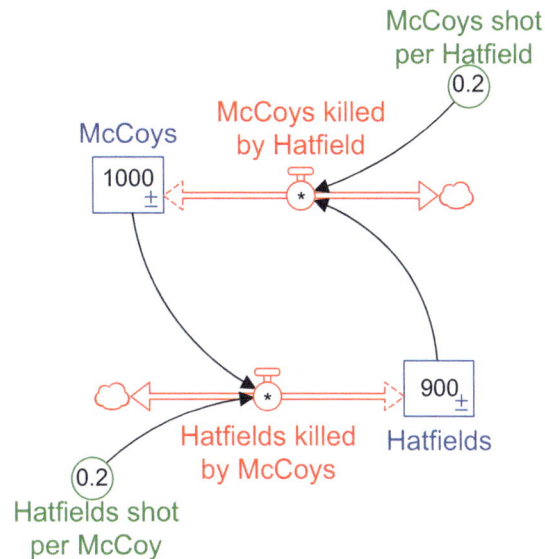

Thoughts and insights from this model:

Experiment with the Model

Now that you've fixed the model you can use it to explore some additional questions. Here are some examples, but feel free to ask your own questions as well.

1. What might be leverage to stop the killing? How could you adjust the model to change the situation, such that the families avoided the need to take revenge?

2. Are there any similar situations that behave in a similar way? Can you relabel and reuse the model in a way that illustrates that new situation?

Challenge 2: Adopting New Technologies

Consider the Story

In 1925, fewer than 50% of US homes had electricity. Of course, today, nearly every home has electricity, whether powered by electrical grids or by alternative energy sources. This graph illustrates how different technologies, including electricity have spread over time. Electricity access is 0% in the early 1900s, then spread to nearly 100% by the end of the century.

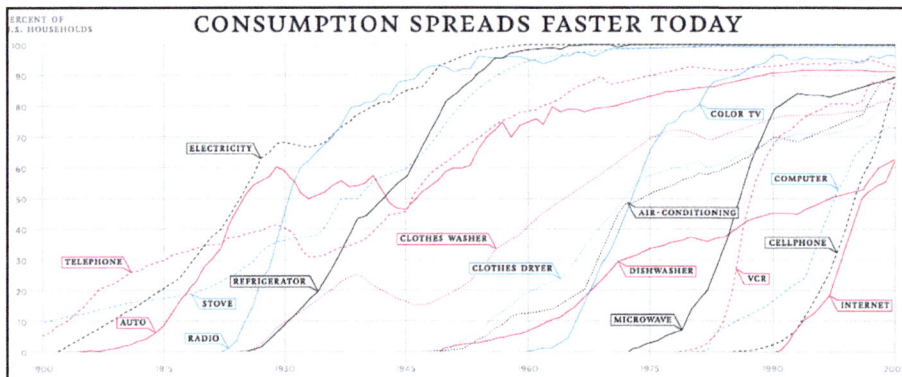

CONSUMPTION SPREADS FASTER TODAY

Nicholas Felton, Used with permission

Over the last 100 years, infrastructure was built in the United States to provide access to almost all households. Now, we hardly even think about it as we switch on the lights. Note that globally, this graph would look different in that access to electricity and other technologies is not universal.

Another resource that's spread in a similar manner to electricity is access to the internet from home. In 1984, essentially no one had access to the internet. Today, that access is over 75%, but leveling off.

Build the Model

Build the model on the next page and insert the numbers and equations as shown. As you build, think about what other model you've built in a previous chapter is similar to this one.

Make sure to input the real world data shown below into the element "Internet household data." This data is based on US Census information from 1997-2012. The earlier data points are guessed, based on general historical information about the origins of the internet. To do this, you'll need to create a graphical function based on time. So each year will have a data point.

Internet_household_data = GRAPH(TIME)
(1984.00, 0.0), (1985.00, 0.0), (1986.00, 0.6), (1987.00, 1.7), (1988.00, 3.0), (1989.00, 3.5), (1990.00, 4.0), (1991.00, 5.0), (1992.00, 6.0), (1993.00, 8.0), (1994.00, 10.0), (1995.00, 13.0), (1996.00, 15.0), (1997.00, 17.0), (1998.00, 18.0), (1999.00, 30.0), (2000.00, 41.5), (2001.00, 45.0), (2002.00, 50.4), (2003.00, 52.0), (2004.00, 54.7), (2005.00, 57.0), (2006.00, 61.7), (2007.00, 68.7), (2008.00, 71.1), (2009.00, 71.3), (2010.00, 71.5), (2011.00, 71.7), (2012.00, 74.8)

Although in reality, the population of the US was growing over this time period, the model uses a constant value for number of US households. The equation for "Total US households" is "Households without internet" + "Households with internet."

As always, make sure your stocks have the non-negative option "unchecked." Since you'll be working to match the model to real data, you'll use the actual years.

Set up the model's "Run Specs" as follows:

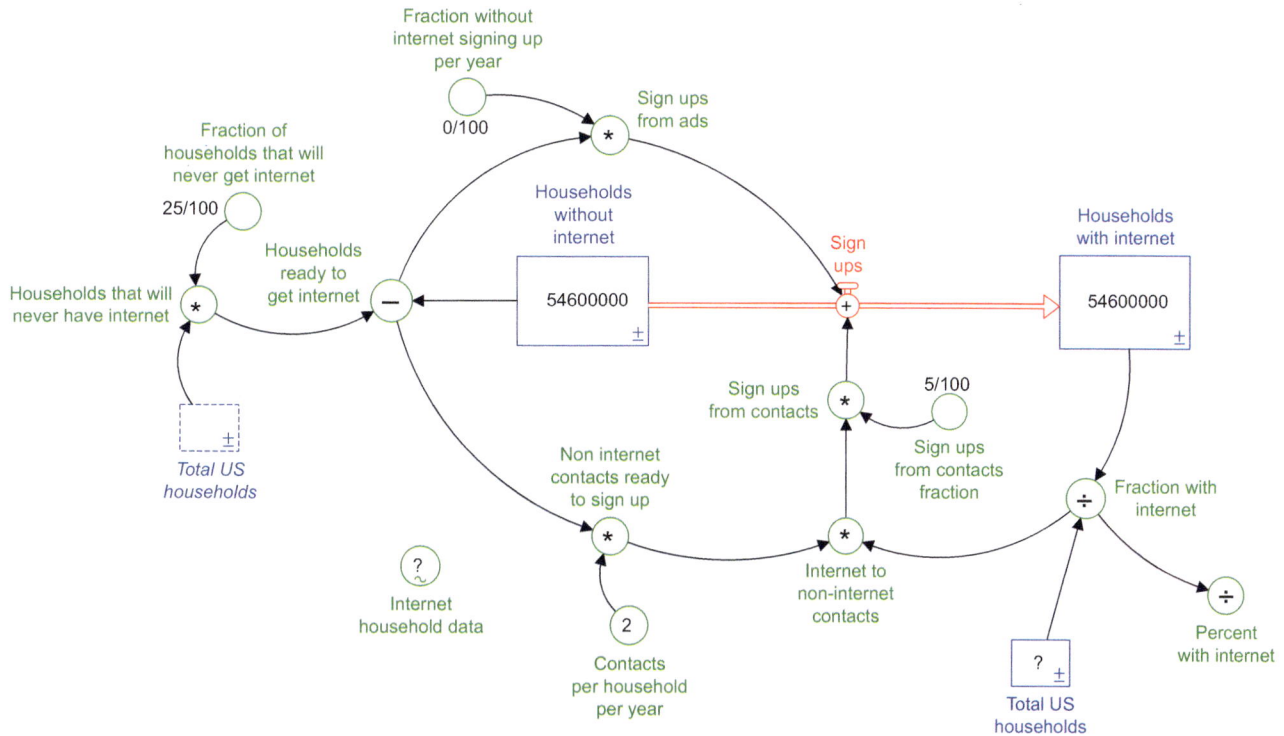

Fraction without internet signing up per year

0/100

Fraction of households that will never get internet

25/100

Sign ups from ads

Households without internet

54600000

Sign ups

Households with internet

54600000

Households that will never have internet

Households ready to get internet

Total US households

Non internet contacts ready to sign up

Sign ups from contacts

5/100

Sign ups from contacts fraction

Fraction with internet

?
~

Internet household data

Contacts per household per year

2

Internet to non-internet contacts

Total US households

Percent with internet

Start Time = 1984
Stop Time = 2012
DT = 0.25 or 1/4
Time Units = Years
Integration Method = Euler

Once you have completed the equations, set up a graph that includes both the "Households with internet" and the "Internet household data." Run the model and check that it is producing the behaviors shown on the graph. If not, check your connections and equations.

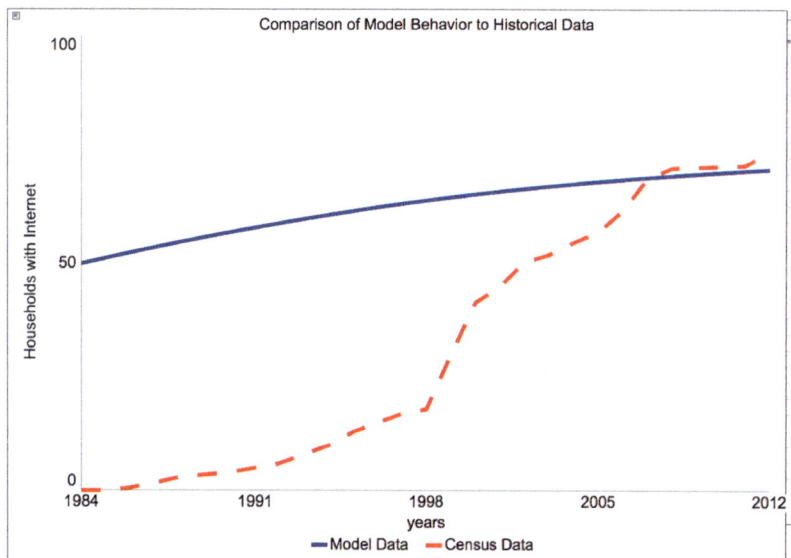

Comparison of Model Behavior to Historical Data

100

50

0
1984   1991   1998   2005   2012
years

Households with Internet

Model Data   Census Data

Fix the Model

Notice that the blue (solid) line on the graph shows the model data. The red (dashed) line shows the census data. The two lines don't match except near the end.

Sometimes it can be helpful to match a model's behavior to real world data. This is called model calibration and helps modelers to validate whether their model structures makes sense. To calibrate the model, you'll need to experiment with changing the starting values of the elements. While doing this, make sure that the total number of households stays the same at 109,200,000 households. The time frame should also remain the same. Adjust any of the constant values or starting values of the stocks.

Your goal is to match the line as closely as possible, realizing that your simulation data will be smoother than the real world data, which will have some bumps in it.

Reflection

How did you adjust the model to create results that most closely matched the real world data? Indicate what you did on the diagram.

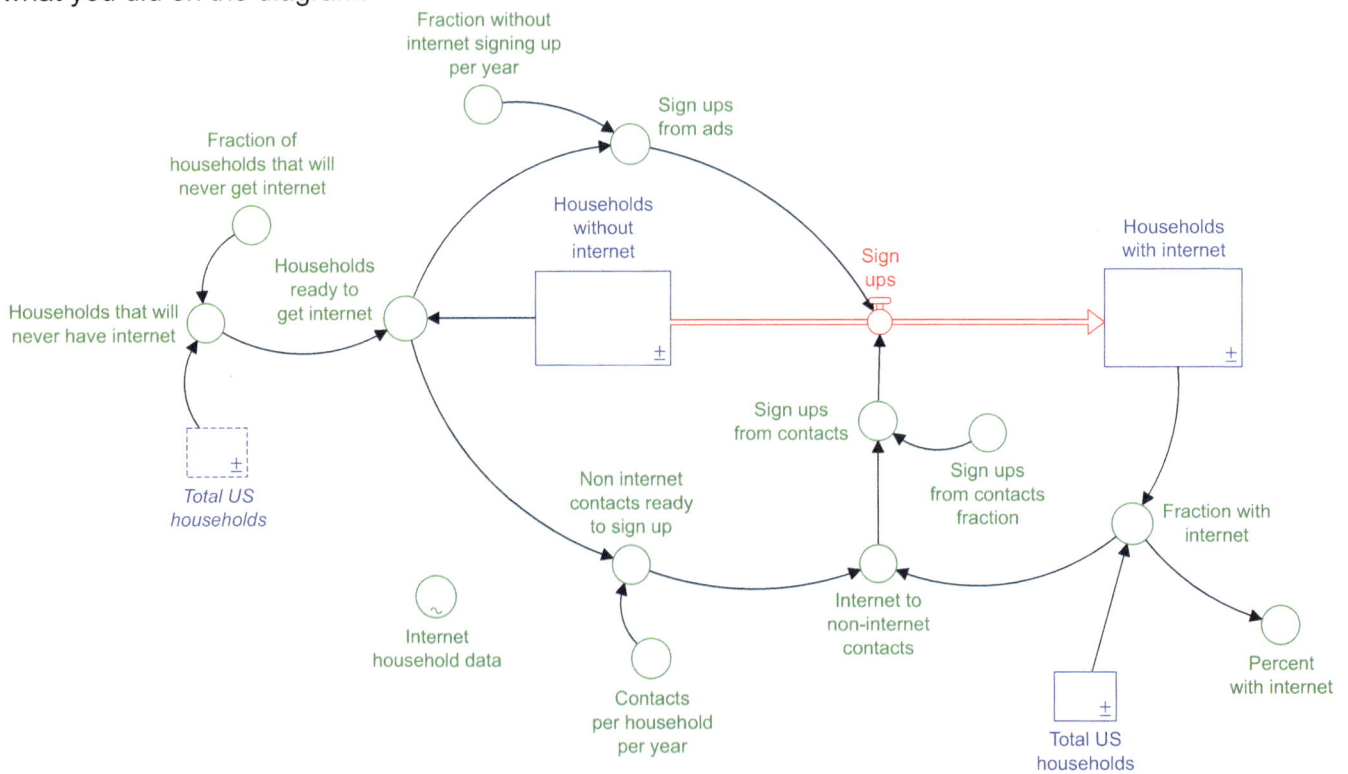

Thoughts and insights from this model:

Experiment with the Model

Now that you've calibrated the model you can use it to explore some additional questions. Here are some examples, but feel free to ask your own questions as well.

1. Compare the impact of "Sign ups from contacts" to the "Sign ups from ads." How are they similar and different? What happens when you adjust the fraction for these two variables?
2. At the beginning when no one had the internet, what had to happen to get the momentum growing of people signing up? How does this strategy connect to efforts to get other new products or ideas to spread?
3. What would affect the "Fraction of households that will never get internet?" Is there a way to represent this on the model to reduce the households that might never sign up?

Dare to Dig Deeper

Further Explorations

One way to build understanding and knowledge of model-building is to seek out and explore models built by other people. You can compare models you find to ones you've built and also to one another.

A few questions to consider as you evaluate models:

1. Do the units make sense? Looks at "An Explanation of Units" in the Appendix B: Equation Helper. Think about whether the modeler has labeled and connected the parts of the model correctly.
2. Does the behavior of the model make sense? For example, make sure that the stocks have the non-negative option unchecked. Do any of the model's stocks go negative in a way that doesn't make sense, e.g., a negative population?
3. Does the time frame make sense for the problem being studied or investigated?
4. Are there missing parts that are important to understanding a particular problem? If yes, how does that limit its usefulness?
5. How can you adjust the model to make sense for a problem you're interested in exploring?

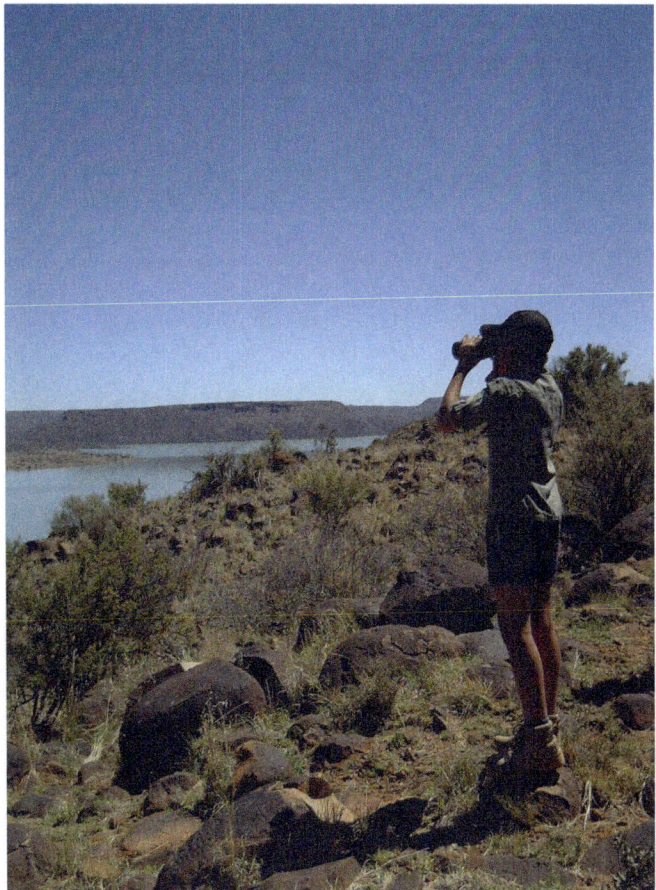

Hiker, Tinus Badenhorst Creative Commons 3.0

Chapter 8:
Endings and Beginnings

My Horse, Brego, Looking for a Path, Anne LaVigne.

Overview

So you've completed all the models and explored many of the connections. What should you do next?

It might seem like simple horse sense, but there's more than one path to follow. Many paths are open to you. Perhaps you already see several avenues to explore. Maybe you don't see any in particular. But in order to continue learning, you must move forward.

A few possibilities are presented in this chapter for you to consider, but exploring on your own can turn up many others. It's time to reach out to see what you can see, and find what you can find. You never know where it might lead.

Recommended Next Steps

The previous chapters were a good starting point for understanding some interesting systems, both fictional and real. Here are a few additional ideas for using the models in the book and for moving to the next step in your learning.

1. Combine Models

The first four chapters each contains a simple model to create and explore. View these as building blocks that you can combine to create more complex models. Think of another situation that might combine the use of two or more of these into one system, and then build a new model of that situation. Here are a few ideas to get you started:

- The acceptance of a new product (Chapter 4) and earnings from its sale (Chapter 1). You can also consider how money earned could contribute to the future success of the product.
- The ability to reach a goal (Chapter 3) based on funding (Chapter 1).
- Creating stuctures to save an endangered species (Chapter 5) based on available funds for the work (Chapter 1).
- Ability to ramp up production of a new product (Chapter 3) and marketing that product, so people who don't currently use it will start (Chapter 4).

2. Replicate and Modify Other People's Models

Use the resources listed in this chapter to find and identify other models that interest you. Then recreate those models, testing and/or modifying them.

3. Complete Further Study

Many of the resources listed have a lot more information about systems than is presented in this book. Some of these are online where you can explore them anytime. Others are more formal written texts.

4. Start with a Blank Page

This option can be difficult, since it's similar to getting out a blank page of paper to start writing a new novel. That said, it can still be fun to explore a new idea. Still, think about whether any of the basic model structures from any of the chapters are useful as a starting point. Most systems will have at least one structure similar to those found in Chapter 1.

Resources

Just do a quick search on the internet, and you'll likely find hundreds of resources connected to systems thinking and dynamic modeling. The ones listed here are a few that have proven useful to the authors, to teachers, to students, and many others. Feel free to explore in any order. Let your interest and curiosity guide you.

The Creative Learning Exchange

This book and accompanying resources are provided through the Creative Learning Exchange (CLE) – http://clexchange.org/

You can find more information about the book and online example models at http://www.clexchange.org/curriculum/modelmysteries/

The CLE website hosts many materials and online resources for K-12 exploration and learning about systems thinking and system dynamics. Among them are:

Road Maps: A Guide to Learning System Dynamics. The System Dynamics in Education Project (SDEP) was carried out by a group of students and staff in the Sloan School of Management at the Massachusetts Institute of Technology, working from 1990 to 2003 under the guidance of Professor Jay W. Forrester, the founder of system dynamics. Together, they created the Road Maps Course. Note that Road Maps materials reference older modeling software versions, and so some technical details may differ. Available at http://www.clexchange.org/curriculum/roadmaps/

System Dynamics in Education: The First Steps - This 59-page illustrated tutorial covers the basics of system dynamics and the use of STELLA II. It serves as a hands-on introduction to system dynamics and student-centered learning for educators and others interested in the basics of system dynamics through computer modeling. Available at https://tinyurl.com/m6zyfxh

Beginner Modeling Exercises - Exercises in modeling constant flows. This compendium of exercises develops understanding of the basic stock-and-flow structure through examples taken from a variety of systems. Available at https://tinyurl.com/lhllt9p

Introduction to Feedback. This document introduces the concepts of reinforcing and balancing feedback within a computer modeling context. Available at https://tinyurl.com/kwzdyyq

Other Resources Focused on Model Creation

The following list includes a few (of many) other organizations providing instruction on the use of system dynamics models.

CC Modeling Systems at http://ccmodelingsystems.com/

This site includes system dynamics examples within math and documentation of student projects for modeling courses along with opportunities for learning.

Massachusetts Institue of Technology (MIT)
  [MIT Sloan School's Learning Edge](https://mitsloan.mit.edu/LearningEdge/system-dynamics/) website at https://mitsloan.mit.edu/LearningEdge/system-dynamics/ includes a variety of case studies, some of which use system dynamics. MIT hosts a [YouTube channel](https://www.youtube.com/user/MITSDM) at https://www.youtube.com/user/MITSDM with videos of how system dynamics models increase understanding of complex issues. MIT also offers its course material online for free, for example, http://ocw.mit.edu/courses/sloan-school-of-management/15-871-introduction-to-system-dynamics-fall-2013/.

U.S. Department of Energy
  Introduction to System Dynamics is an online book that introduces system dynamics, a powerful methodology for framing, understanding, and discussing complex policy issues and problems. Available at https://web.nmsu.edu/~lang/files/mike.pdf

Additional Written Texts
These texts are written primarily for people studying system dynamics in college, but some have wider audiences, e.g., teachers and other interested individuals.

Fisher, Diana (2005, 2011). *Lessons in Mathematics: A Dynamic Approach* and *Modeling Dynamic Systems: Lessons for a First Course* (third edition)
  http://www.iseesystems.com/store/books/diana-fisher-set/

Ford, Andrew. (2010). *Modeling the Environment* (second edition)
  http://www.amazon.com/Modeling-Environment-Second-Andrew-Ford/dp/1597264733

Meadows, Donella H. (2008). *Thinking in Systems, A Primer* (White River Junction, VT: Chelsea Green Publishing): http://www.chelseagreen.com/bookstore/item/thinking_in_systems:paperback

Richmond, Barry. *The "Thinking" In Systems Thinking: Seven Essential Skills*. ISBN 188382348x.

Sterman, John. (2000). *Business Dynamics: Systems Thinking and Modeling for a Complex World*. ISBN 0072311355.

Appendix A: Creating Model Elements Using Stella

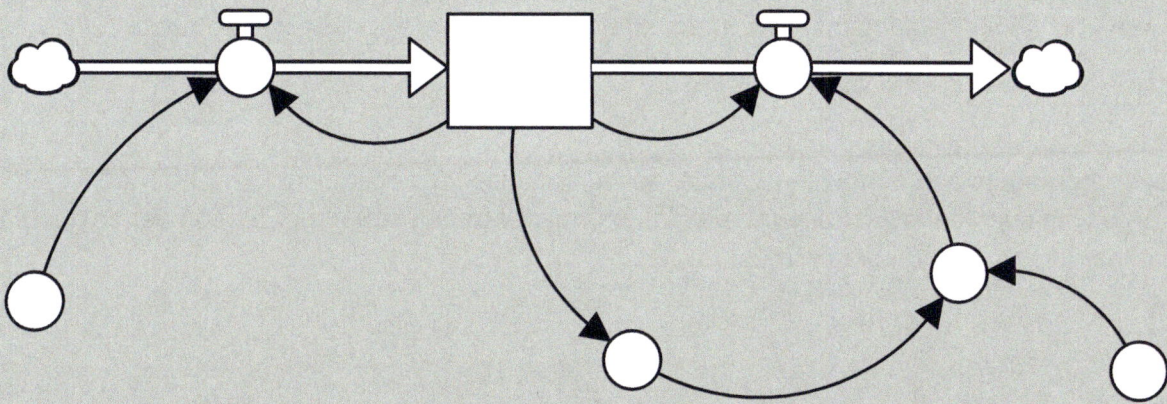

Overview

Never used a modeling software program before? This section describes basic building blocks to create a model (or picture) of a system. A model represents how a system works, but it isn't the system itself. All models in the book are created using Stella by isee systems, inc., although other modeling software is available. See Appendix B: Equation Helper.

Model Parts

These are the main model parts in Stella that are needed for creating a basic model.

☐ Stock

A stock represents an amount you want to track in a model. It's an accumulation. It can be concrete, like the number of trees in a forest or abstract, like an amount of happiness. Click the icon and then click again on your model page to create a new stock. Then just type in a name.

⟨⟩ Flow – Uniflow vs. Biflow

Flows go into and out from stocks. The "stuff" of a stock can only get there through a flow. A flow is kind of like a river flowing. Some rivers flow fast, while others move very slowly. Flows work in a similar way, showing how fast "stuff" moves in or out of a stock. A uniflow can only move "stuff" in one direction. A biflow (shown here) can move "stuff" in both directions. When creating a biflow, make sure to draw it in the correct direction, as indicated. Otherwise, the model will not create the expected behavior.

◯ Converter

A converter represents part of how the system works, but it isn't a stock. It contains information which is passed onto whatever it affects. For example, the number of trees planted per person per day could be a converter that affects the number of trees.

↗ Connector

Connectors show how elements affect one another. For example, the number of trees planted per person per day could affect the number of new seedlings in a forest.

👻 Ghost (not available in Stella Online)

A ghost is simply a duplicate of another element in your model. The main reason for creating a ghost is to avoid having crossed lines in your model which can look confusing and messy. One goal of modeling is to communicate clearly how something works. Given that, it's important to keep your model clear of crossed lines.

📈 Graph

Graphs show what happens to model elements over time. Generally, you'll want to create a graph to show what's happening to the stocks. Click the box for Comparative to see all runs on the same graph.

🔢 Numeric display (not available in Stella Online)

A numeric display shows the actual value of an element. Usually, you'll create a numeric display to see the final value of a stock at the end of a run.

▦ Table (not available in Stella Online)

Tables show the numeric values of model elements throughout an entire run. (not available in Stella)

Equations and Settings

These are the main functions needed to create the math behind the model.

 **Apply**

After entering an equation, click the green check mark to confirm.

◀ **Drawer Open and** ▷ **Drawer Close**

Use this triangle to open and close the sidebar on the right, where you can enter equations and other settings.

Edit Mode vs. **Explore Mode**

Use Edit Mode when creating a model. Use Explore Mode when running and testing a model.

x^2 **Equation**

Click this icon in the side panel to enter an equation or value for a model part. To create most of the equations, you'll just need to use basic math symbols and the variables that are part of your model. So, if you see a plus (+) sign, that means you'll need to add the variables that are affecting that variable with the plus sign. Use these basic symbols:

| Add + | Subtract − | Multiply * | Divide ÷ |

x^2 **Model View vs.** 🌐 **Map View**

Clicking these icons in the top menu switches between the model (with numbers/equations) and the map (no numbers/equations).

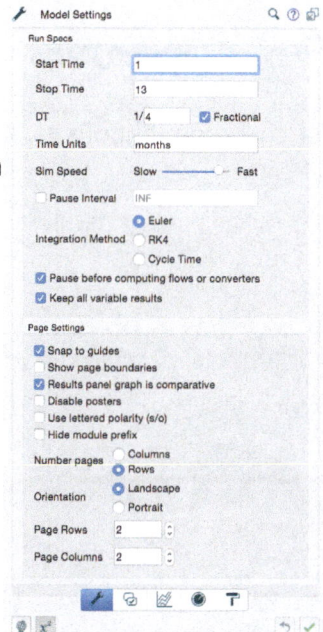

🔧 **Model Settings** (see window at right)

1. Start Time and Stop Time – This is how long the model will run.
2. DT (delta time) – DT is how often the model will calculate model values each time unit. A small DT (e.g., 1/32) means that the model will determine new data points 32 times in each time unit. A large DT (e.g., 1/2) means that the model will determine new data points only 2 times in each time unit.
3. Time Units – This can be set to days, months or years. It's very important to keep your time units the same throughout the model.
4. Integration Method – Use the method recommended for each of the models. Generally, you can use Euler for the simpler models. Switch to RK4 for more complex models, e.g., a predator/prey model.

Style (not available with Stella Online)

Set fonts, colors and sizes using the Style screen.

↶ **Undo**

This icon will undo one action.

Viewing and Running the Model

These are the main functions needed to view and run the model.

Note: to save your model, use the File menu --> Save.

❚❚ Pause

Similar to watching a video, use the pause button to stop a model in the middle with the option to continue to run it.

▶ Play

Similar to watching a video, use the play button to run a model over the time period you determined. When the model runs, it shows what happens to the system over time. It's important to have a graph created, so you can see the dynamics.

⊕ Plus and ⊖ Minus

Use the plus and minus signs to add variables to a graph or table.

↶ Restore

The restore button returns all the model values and graphs to their original settings.

■ Stop

Similar to watching a video, use the stop button to end a model run.

🔎⊕ Zoom In and 🔎⊖ Zoom Out

Use the zoom buttons to increase or decrease the size of the model icons.

Appendix B: Equation Helper with an Explanation of Units

Overview

This section includes a description of available modeling software. It also contains helpful hints for completing the main model for each chapter and some guidance for exploring the Dares. If the behavior of your model does not match the graph(s) shown, use this section to check your model's equations and connections. You can also find some key questions to ask yourself to check accuracy.

In addition, example models are available online to show possible ways to represent the additional stories. These are intended to provide inspiration and guidance, rather than represent "right answers" to any given storyline and are not essential for you to explore on your own.

Modeling Software Options

Note that many software options exist. These are just a few that the authors have personally used to create models. This list is not meant as a endorsement of any particular option. The authors chose Stella to illustrate this book (*Model Mysteries*), but another option may work better for any given reader. Visit the book's webpage for additional information at http://www. clexchange.org/curriculum/modelmysteries/

Stella – https://iseesystems.com/

> isee systems, inc. distributes Stella and other system dynamics products. A free, limited, online version is available that will work for building all the models in the book. Find additional info about Stella Online at https://www.iseesystems. com/store/products/stella-online.aspx

Other Options:

Splash - http://www.clexchange.org/splash/

> Splash (original, free version for mobile devices) and SplashX (version for laptops and desktops) are visual modeling tools that emphasize fun, delight, and ease-of-use. These are potential options for building most of the models in the book.

Insight Maker – https://insightmaker.com/

> Insight Maker is a free, online modeling option to create system dynamics models.

Vensim PLE – http://vensim.com/

> Vensim PLE is system dynamics modeling software, free for personal learning and education.

General Questions, Checks, and Notes

1. What is the DT set to? Did you set it as indicated for this model?
2. What are the start and stop times? Did you run the model for the full time period?
3. What integration method is being used? Is it set correctly?
4. Check your flows.
   - Did you create the correct type of flow(s), i.e., uniflow or biflow?
   - Are your flows connected to the stocks? If you do not see the expected behavior, make sure that your flows are connected to the stock. You can test this by moving the stock around on the screen, making sure that the flows do not become disconnected in the process. If a flow is disconnected, drag the end of the flow over until it touches the stock and connects.
5. Check all your equations. When a mathematical operation is shown, e.g., addition(+), subtraction(−), multiplication (*), or division(÷ or /), make sure that you have the variables connected as shown.
6. Is the graph scaled correctly? Check numbers on the graph axes to make sure they match what you see in the book. In some modeling software, you can change the scales to be automatic or set by you.
7. What software are you using? These models were created with Stella, but other software may show you slightly different graph results. The numbers should match, though.
8. Notice that the equations in this section show underlines where the model parts have spaces. For example, Dodo population would be shown as Dodo_population. You do not need to type in the underlines when you add parts or create equations. The software may do this for you as part of its programming.

Additional Online Resources

The availability of new resources and editions will be announced in the CLE Newsletter. You can also find them on the Model Mysteries webpage: http://www.clexchange.org/curriculum/modelmysteries/

Please send any suggestions for resources that would help you complete the mysteries in the book to: webmaster@clexchange.org.

Chapter 1: Growing, Growing, Gone

Base Model 1 Equations
Zombie Chickens
    INIT Zombie_chickens = 1
Replicating_ZCs = 2
Curing_ZCs = 0

Base Model 2 Equations
Zombie Chickens
    INIT Zombie_chickens = 1
    INFLOWS:
        Replicating_ZCs = Replication_rate*Zombie_chickens
    OUTFLOWS:
        Curing_ZCs = Cure_rate*Zombie_chickens
Cure_rate = 0
Replication_rate = 0.5

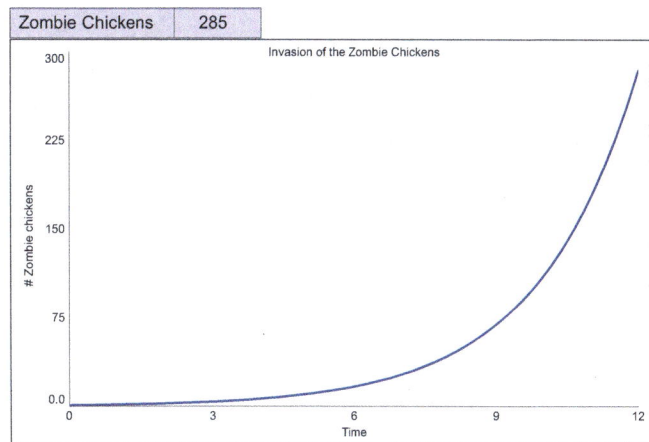

Expected behavior for second base model

Expected behavior
Assuming that all equations are entered correctly, and that the model is set to run for 12 months, you should see this behavior on the graph. It's called exponential growth because it grows slowly at first, then speeds up over time.

Troubleshooting
This model's equations use only multiplication (*) to calculate the rates that the ZCs increase and decrease. If you do not see the expected behavior, make sure that your flows are connected to the stock.

Dare
The equations for the first dare are exactly the same as the original ZC model, but you'll need to increase the time that the model runs. To have the population of ZCs exceed the Earth's population, the model will need to run for 50 months.

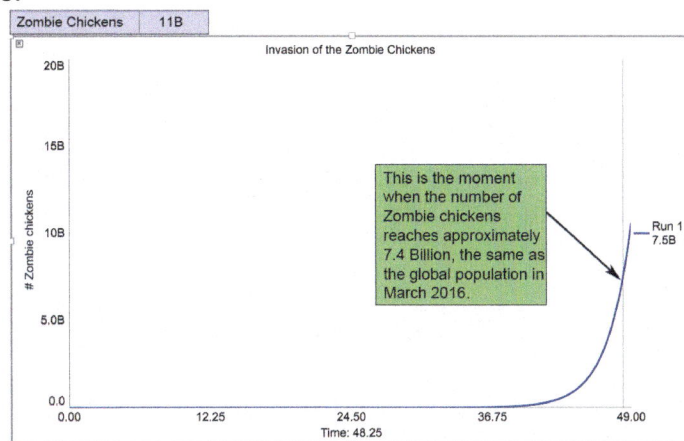

This is the moment when the number of Zombie chickens reaches approximately 7.4 Billion, the same as the global population in March 2016.

Expected behavior for first dare

Double Dare

There is no one right answer to this dare. However, the key to preventing the ZC takeover is to set the numbers so the inflow is smaller than the outflow. In that way, the ZCs are cured faster than they can reproduce, and the number of ZCs would go down.

Triple Dog Dare

The model becomes more complicated when it takes time to develop a cure. Of course, this is more realistic, since cures do not magically appear instantaneously. The key then is to develop the cure and then get the cure rate to be higher than the replication rate. Otherwise, the ZCs will continue to rise or possibly just level off.

The graph here shows what happens if the cure is developed after 10 months and has a "Cure rate" of 50%. In reality, even if the cure was developed and ready to go, it would take time to start using it. To keep the model simple, we are not including those conditions in this model. Later chapters in the book will show how to add a time delay.

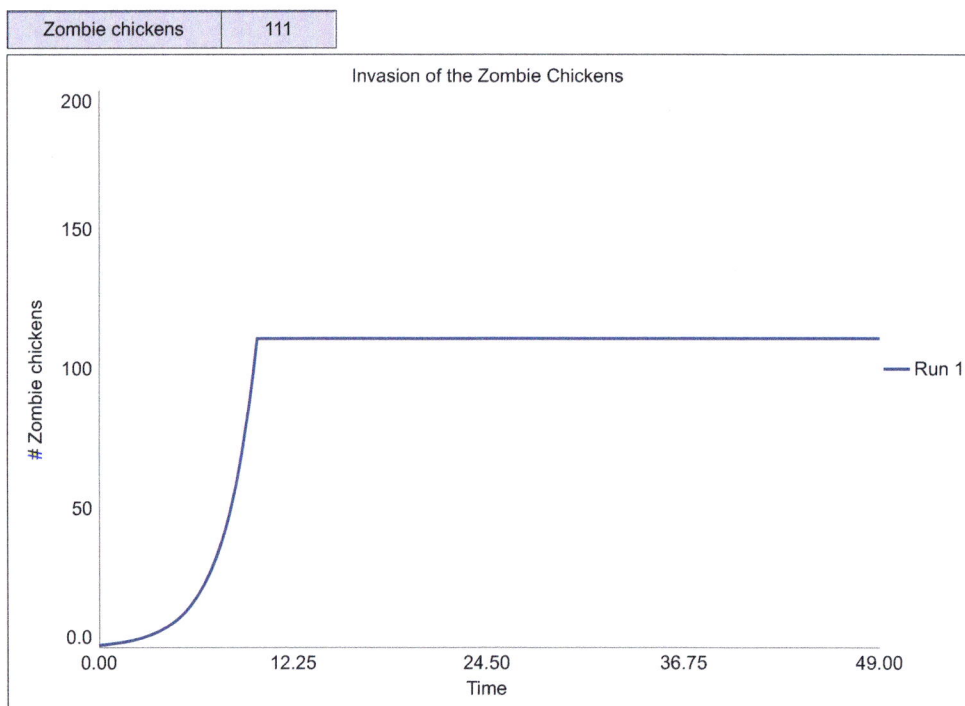

Zombie chickens	111

Expected behavior when settings indicate 10-month time delay for cure

How could you create a different result, given the same 10-month delay? As the situation stands, people would have to continue to work to cure the ZCs forever.

Full Models

Note: To see a completed, running model of this and all other models in the book, visit "Models Mysteries: Check Your Models" at http://www.clexchange.org/curriculum/modelmysteries/MM_models

Full Models

Chapter 2: Energy Drink Mania

Base Model Equations

Mg_caffeine_in_body
  INIT Mg_caffeine_in_body = 0
  INFLOWS:
    Absorption_per_hour = Mg_caffeine_in_stomach/Absorption_time
  OUTFLOWS:
    Elimination_per_hour = Mg_caffeine_in_body/elimination_time
Mg_caffeine_in_stomach
  INIT Mg_caffeine_in_stomach = 0
  INFLOWS:
    Intake_per_hour = Cans_per_hour*Mg_caffeine_per_can
  OUTFLOWS:
    Absorption_per_hour = Mg_caffeine_in_stomach/Absorption_time
Absorption_time = 1
Cans_per_hour = GRAPH(TIME)
(0.00, 0.000), (1.00, 0.000), (2.00, 0.000), (3.00, 0.000), (4.00, 1.000), (5.00, 1.000), (6.00, 1.000), (7.00, 1.000), (8.00, 0.000), (9.00, 0.000), (10.00, 0.000), (11.00, 0.000), (12.00, 0.000), (13.00, 0.000), (14.00, 0.000), (15.00, 0.000), (16.00, 0.000), (17.00, 0.000), (18.00, 0.000), (19.00, 0.000), (20.00, 0.000), (21.00, 0.000), (22.00, 0.000), (23.00, 0.000), (24.00, 0.000)
Elimination_time = 11
Mg_caffeine_per_can = 100

Expected Behavior

Assuming that all equations are entered correctly, and that the model is set to run for 24 hours, you should see this behavior on the graph. It shows a fast increase in caffeine levels as you consume energy drinks but a slow decline, faster at first and slower at the end. This is called exponential decay.

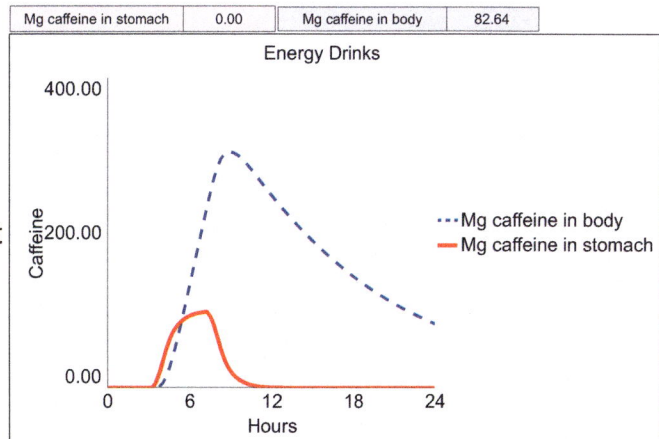

Expected behavior for base model

Troubleshooting

Two variables have a ÷ sign. In modeling software, division is indicated with a slash (/). It's important that the variables are divided correctly. For example, the "Absorption per hour" is determined by the "Mg caffeine in stomach" divided by the "Absorption time." This shows that if it takes an average time to eliminate caffeine, but that the more there is in the stomach, the more will be absorbed. It works in a similar way for "Elimination time." Also make sure that your flows are connected to the stock.

Dare

The equations for the first dare are exactly the same as the original energy drink model, but you'll need to increase the time that the model runs. Given the original settings for "Cans per hour," it takes about 48 hours for the level of caffeine in the body to drop below 10 mg. When considering how many energy drinks to consume, some would argue that the best choice would be none. That said, you can evaluate many different aspects of the issue, for example, recommended maximum caffeine intake by age, short and long-term effects of consuming caffeine, personal safety if driving a car when tired, and potential effects of consuming other additives in energy drinks.

Double Dare

There is no one right answer to this dare, but here is one partial solution. The "Cans per hour" starts high, and then goes down quickly. Even then, by hour 18, the levels are still at around 70 mg in the body. It's not until the end, when the caffeine level is below 50 mg.

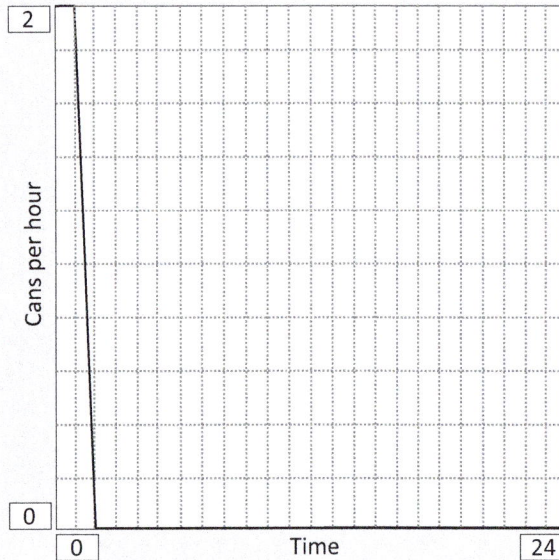

Graphical function for Double Dare

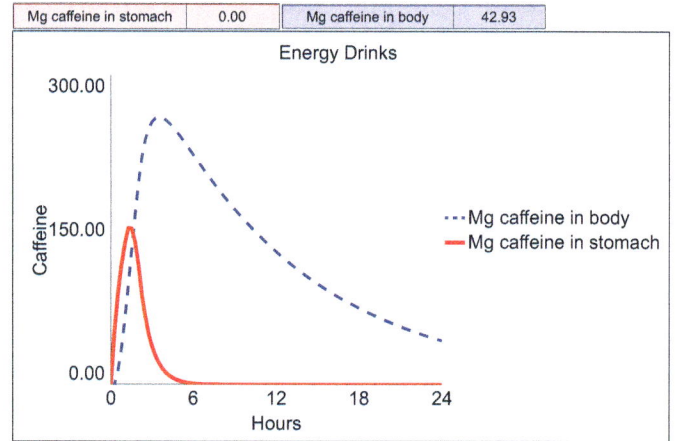

Model results for Double Dare

Triple Dog Dare

Again, there's no one solution here. Here is one option showing a low level of "Cans per hour" over a longer period of time.

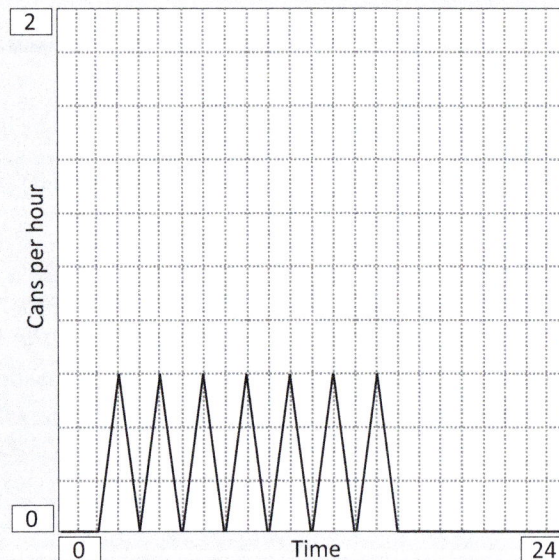

Graphical function for Triple Dog Dare

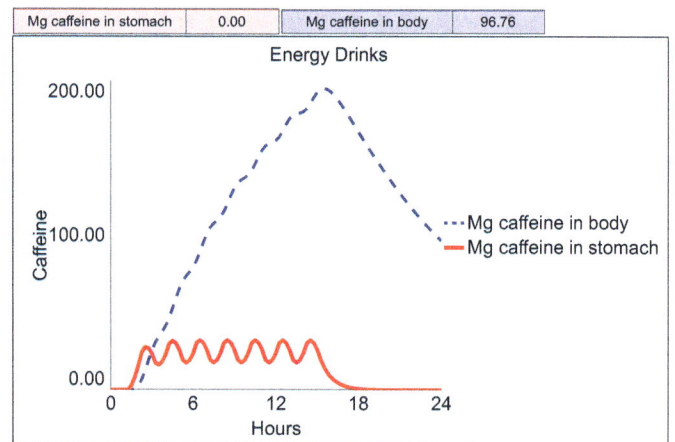

Model results for Triple Dog Dare

Chapter 3: Mind the Gap

Base Model Equations
Production_capacity
   INIT Production_capacity = 10000
   INFLOWS: Changing_capacity = Capacity_gap/Time_to__ramp_up_production
Capacity_gap = Capacity_goal-Production_capacity
Capacity_goal = 1E6
Time_to_ramp_up_production = 52

Expected Behavior
Assuming that all equations are entered correctly, and that the model is set to run for 12 months, you should see this behavior on the graph. The "Production capacity" is growing quickly, since the gap is so large at the beginning.

Production capacity	214k

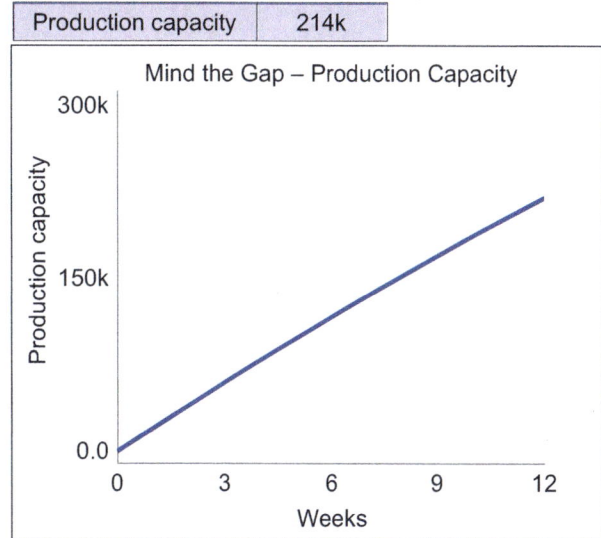

Expected behavior for the base model

Troubleshooting
One variable has a ÷ sign. In modeling software, division is indicated with a slash (/). It's important that the variable is divided correctly. The "Changing capacity" is determined by the "Capacity gap" divided by the "Time to ramp up production." This shows that if it takes a year to ramp up production, you'd be able to produce 1/52 (one week's worth) in any given week. Also make sure that your flows are connected to the stock.

Dare
The equations for the first dare are exactly the same as the original model, but you'll need to increase the time that the model runs. The model never really reaches the goal of one million for "Production capacity," since the "Changing capacity" is always a fraction of the gap. To get over 999,000, though, the model must run for at least 360 weeks. This shows that as you get closer to reaching a goal, there's a tendency do less. To increase growth again, you must set a higher goal.

Production capacity	999,041

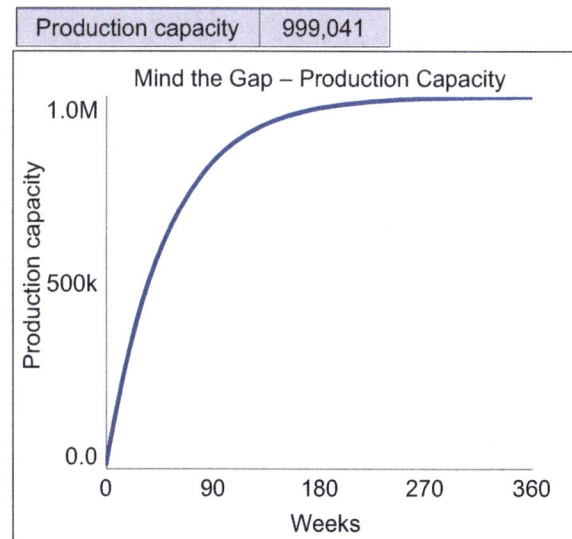

Expected behavior for first dare

Double Dare
There is no one right answer to this dare. If concerned people lived in this world with someone like Vic Schuss, they might consider ways to disrupt his plans. These might include ways to stop him from increasing his capacity. For example, if he needed to build a bigger factory to create more production lines, concerned citizens might work to stop him from obtaining the needed materials. In the model, this would likely increase the time needed to ramp up production.

Triple Dog Dare

The model becomes a bit more complicated when you consider the issue of distribution. Every time a new stock is added, a delay is created. So it takes time for the stuff in the stock to change. In this case, it takes time to build up the "Production capacity" and it takes time to distribute the actual devices, once they're produced. This model shows one way to represent that.

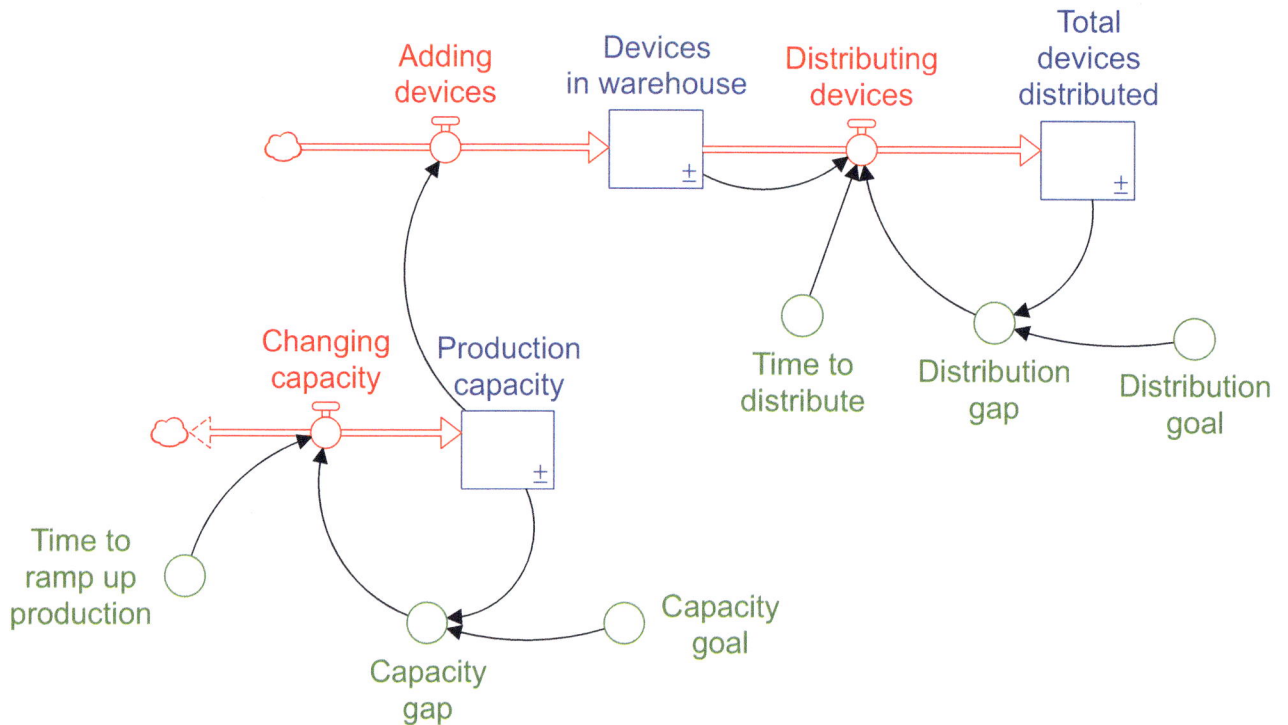

Equations

Devices_in_warehouse
   INIT Devices_in_warehouse = 1
   INFLOWS:
      Adding_devices = Production_capacity
   OUTFLOWS:
      Distributing_devices = min(Distribution_gap/Time_to_distribute, Devices_in_warehouse/Time_to_distribute)

Production_capacity
   INIT Production_capacity = 10000
   INFLOWS:
      Changing_capacity = Capacity_gap/Time_to_ramp_up_production

Total_devices_distributed
   INIT Total_devices_distributed = 1
   INFLOWS:
      Distributing_devices = min(Distribution_gap/Time_to_distribute, Devices_in_warehouse/Time_to_distribute)

Capacity_gap = Capacity_goal-Production_capacity

Capacity_goal = 1000000

Distribution_gap = Distribution_goal-Total_devices_distributed

Distribution_goal = 6000000000

Time_to_distribute = 12

Time_to_ramp_up_production = 52

The "Changing capacity" affects the "Production capacity," which then affects how many are added to the warehouse for distribution each week. How many devices are actually distributed depends on both the goal and how many are actually available in the warehouse. If the warehouse does not have enough, the distribution is limited to the number in stock.

With this model, you can explore what happens if you increase or decrease the "Time" or "Goal" variables. The graph below shows only a small number of the desired six billion devices have been distributed after almost seven years. Try to determine how to actually distribute six billion devices in a reasonable amount of time.

Again, with this more complicated model you can explore how to stop Vic Schuss. Now there are multiple places to prevent him from producing and distributing his devices.

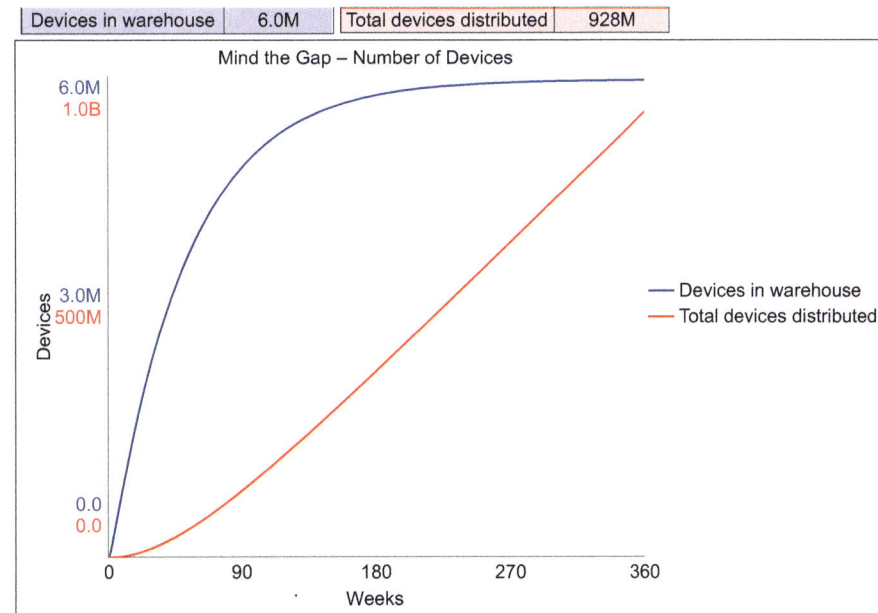

| Devices in warehouse | 6.0M | Total devices distributed | 928M |

Mind the Gap – Number of Devices

Devices in warehouse
Total devices distributed

Expected behavior with new structure and two stocks

Of course other questions to ask are "What's missing in this model?" and "What other leverage could be added?" For example, would educating people about the dangers stop them from accepting the "gift" from Vic in the first place?

Chapter 4: Spreading Like Crazy

Base Model Equations

Members
   INIT Members = 1
   INFLOWS:
      People_joining = Contacts_between_members_and_nonmembers*Likelihood_of_spread
NonMembers
   INIT NonMembers = Total_people-Members
Contacts_per_member_per_month = 10
Contacts_between_members_and_nonmembers = NonMember_fraction*Member_Contacts_per_month
Likelihood_of_spread = .1
Member_contacts_per_month = Members*Contacts_per_member_per_month
NonMember_fraction = NonMembers/Total_people
Total_people = 1000000

Expected Behavior

Assuming that all equations are entered correctly, and that the model is set to run for 12 months, you should see this behavior on the graph. The "Members" are just starting to grow, seemingly very slowly.

Members	43k	NonMembers	957k

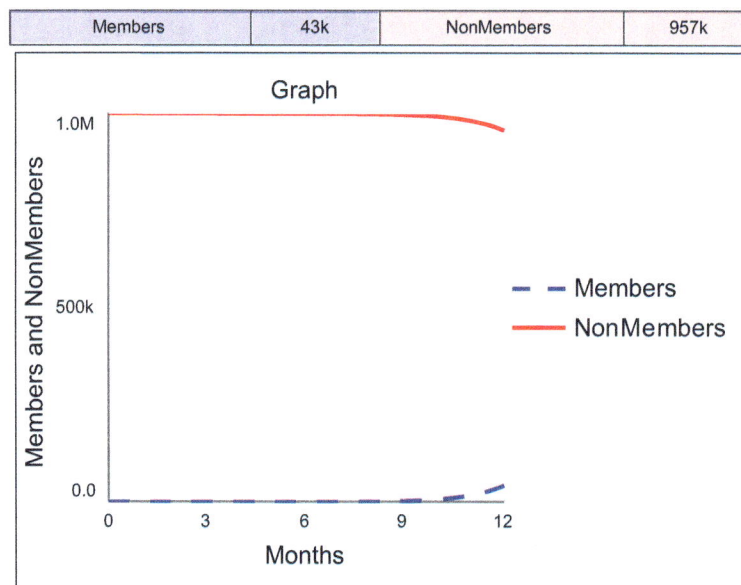

Expected behavior the base model

Troubleshooting

One variable has a ÷ sign. In modeling software, division is indicated with a slash (/). It's important that the variable is divided correctly. The "NonMember fraction" is determined by the "NonMembers" divided by the "Total people." This shows the fraction of the population that have not yet become "Members."

Dare

Assuming that all equations are entered correctly, and that you extend the model to run for 24 months, you should see this behavior on the graph. The "Members" grow in a similar way to the "Zombie chickens" in Chapter 1 at first. Then, as the number of people who are "NonMembers" decreases, the number of "Members" levels off. It's called s-shaped growth because it looks like the letter 's.' Something grows slowly at first, then speeds up, then levels off.

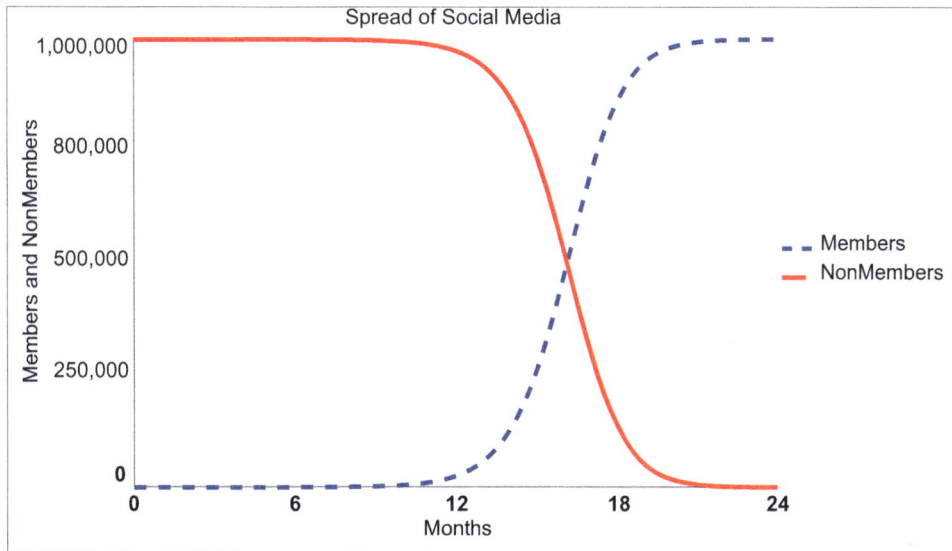

Expected behavior for first dare

Double Dare

There is no one right answer to this dare. In trying to get a new idea to spread, (like for this model, getting new members to join a social media site), there are three main variables you can change:

"Likelihood of spread" – A high percent for this factor might mean that the site is very engaging and fun. The site developers increase investment in creating and updating the site over time to make sure it stays attractive to potential new members.

"Contacts per member per month" – A high number here could indicate that the current "Members" are very happy and are choosing to share the site with others a lot.

"Total people" – This variable is really your potential audience. You can't count everyone in the world, since some of them don't use social media at all, e.g., babies. You can consider how to expand the possible audience by broadening the appeal for different groups, e.g., people who speak various languages.

Triple Dog Dare

Many ways exist to take on this dare. The map shows the simplest possible representation, with the only outflow being people who leave after joining. This means that once people leave, they don't come back.

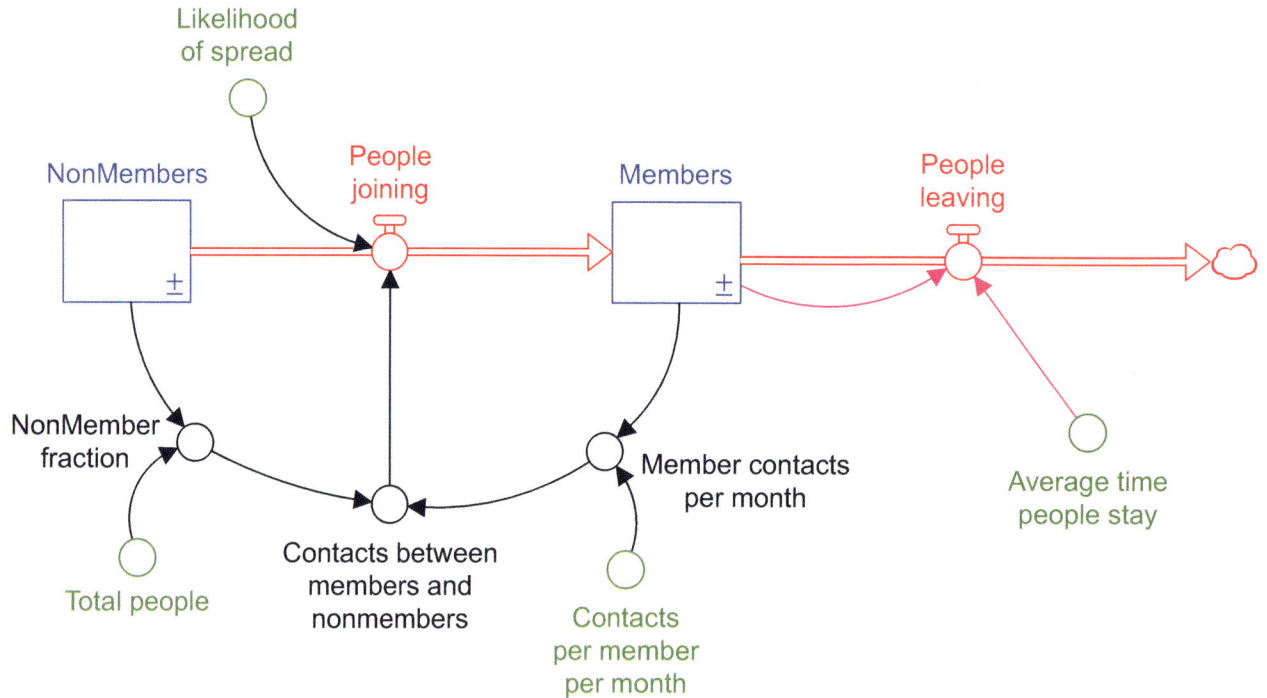

Equations (note that equations added to base model are italicized in red)

Members
    INIT Members = 1
    INFLOWS:
        People__joining = Contacts_between_members_and_nonmembers*Likelihood_of_spread
    OUTFLOWS:
        People_leaving = Members/Average_time_people_stay
NonMembers
    INIT NonMembers = Total_people-Members
    OUTFLOWS:
        People__joining = Contacts_between_members_and_nonmembers*Likelihood_of_spread
Average_time_people_stay = 10
Contacts__per_member_per_month = 10
Contacts_between__members_and__nonmembers = NonMember_fraction*Member_Contacts_per_month
Likelihood_of_spread = .1
Member_contacts_per_month = Members*Contacts__per_member_per_month
NonMember_fraction = NonMembers/Total_people
Total_people = 1000000

The behavior of this model is shown below. Notice that the membership on the site grows for awhile and then declines. What can be done about this problem? Given that this part of the puzzle is indeed a real issue for typical social media sites, how can you influence how long people stay?

Members	501k	NonMembers	4.2k

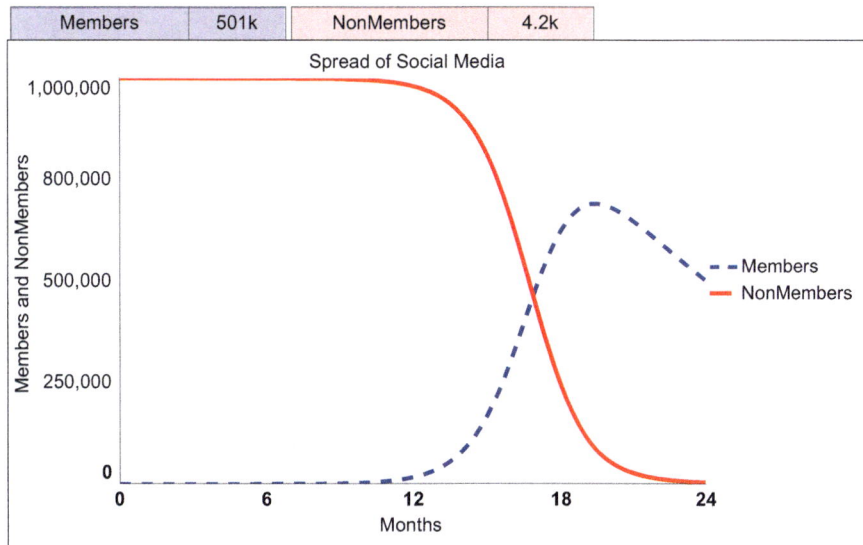

Expected behavior with people leaving on average after 10 months

What's missing in this model? You could choose to do something different, for example, having the flow of people leaving go back into the stock of "NonMembers" rather than into a cloud, never to be seen again. This would mean that you could attract them again to join. You'd have to decide whether or not that is a realistic situation, given your own experience with social media sites you've left.

Chapter 5: The Disappeared

Base Model 1 Equations

Population
  INIT Population = 500
  INFLOWS:
    Births = Population*Birth_fraction
  OUTFLOWS:
    Deaths = Population/Actual_lifespan
Resources
  INIT Resources = 50000
Actual_lifespan = Average_lifespan*Impact_on_lifespan
Average_lifespan = 50
Birth_fraction = .02
Impact_on_lifespan = GRAPH(resources_per_person/Resources_needed_per_person)
(0.000, 0.000), (0.100, 0.185), (0.200, 0.405), (0.300, 0.560), (0.400, 0.700), (0.500, 0.825), (0.600, 0.920), (0.700, 0.975), (0.800, 1.000), (0.900, 1.000), (1.000, 1.000)
Resources_needed_per_person = 1
resources_per_person = Resources/Population

Base Model 2 Equations

Population
  INIT Population = 500
  INFLOWS:
    Births = Population*Birth_fraction
  OUTFLOWS:
    Deaths = Population/Actual_lifespan
Resources
  INIT Resources = Max_resources
  INFLOWS:
    Regenerating = (Max_resources-Resources)/Regeneration_time
  OUTFLOWS:
    Using = MIN(Desired_annual_use, Max_use_per_year)
Actual_lifespan = Average_lifespan*Impact_on_lifespan
Average_lifespan = 50
Birth_fraction = .02
Desired_annual_use = Population*Resources_needed_per_person
Impact_on_lifespan = GRAPH(resources_per_person/Resources_needed_per_person)
(0.000, 0.000), (0.100, 0.185), (0.200, 0.405), (0.300, 0.560), (0.400, 0.700), (0.500, 0.825), (0.600, 0.920), (0.700, 0.975), (0.800, 1.000), (0.900, 1.000), (1.000, 1.000)
Max_resources = 50000
Max_use_per_year = Resources/Quickest_use_of_resources
Quickest_use_of_resources = 1
Regeneration_time = GRAPH(Resources_to_max)
(0.000, 89.00), (0.100, 55.00), (0.200, 34.00), (0.300, 21.00), (0.400, 13.00), (0.500, 8.00), (0.600, 5.00), (0.700, 3.00), (0.800, 2.00), (0.900, 1.00), (1.000, 1.00)

Resources_needed_per_person = 1
resources_per_person = Resources/Population
Resources_to_max = Resources/Max_resources

Expected behavior

Assuming that all equations are entered correctly, you should see this behavior on the graph. It's called steady state, which shows that all the variables are set in a way that produces no change over time.

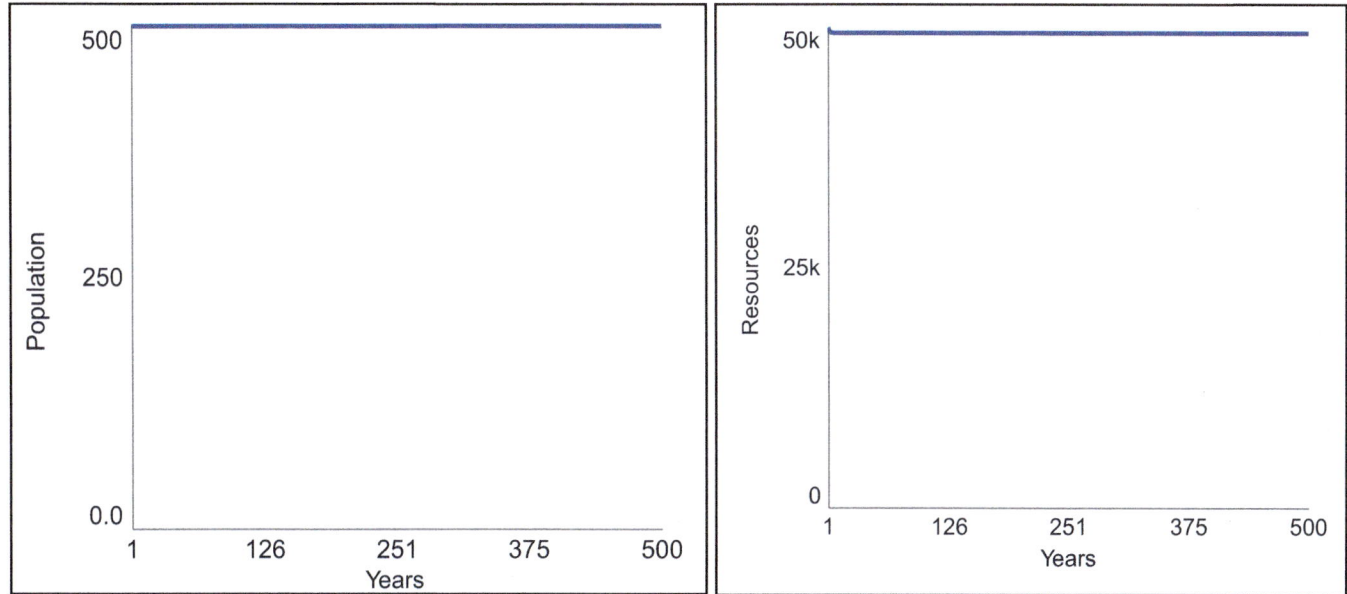

Expected behavior for second base model

Troubleshooting

If you do not see the expected behavior, make sure that your flows are connected to the stocks as shown. Also check all equations and, in particular, the points on the graphical functions. If these numbers are not input as indicated, you could see very different behavior.

Dare

The equations for the first dare are exactly the same as the original model, but you'll need to increase the average lifespan to 75 years. The graphs below show the expected behavior for both the "Population" and the "Resources." As the population grows exponentially, more and more resources are used. Eventually, the use overwhelms the regeneration of the resources, and the population crashes too.

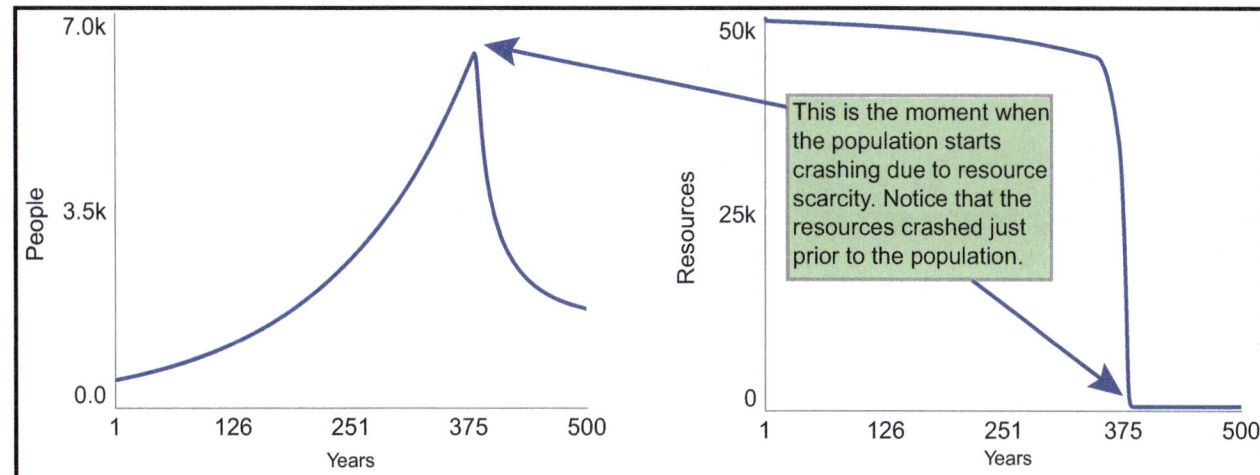

This is the moment when the population starts crashing due to resource scarcity. Notice that the resources crashed just prior to the population.

Expected behavior for first dare

Double Dare

There is no one right answer to this dare, however, one key insight is to realize that the resources will decline, eventually leading to a population crash, unless the births are lower than the deaths.

Triple Dog Dare

Trying to find an acceptable solution to the resource depletion/population crash is challenging to say the least. One issue is that people have very different ideas about how to do this, and what some people see as a solution, others may find immoral. Shown here is one such course of action that some people may find unethical. Simply, this adjustment adds an impact to the births side of the model, similar to the structure that affects lifespan. It shows that if the resource availability goes down, the birth fraction will also go down.

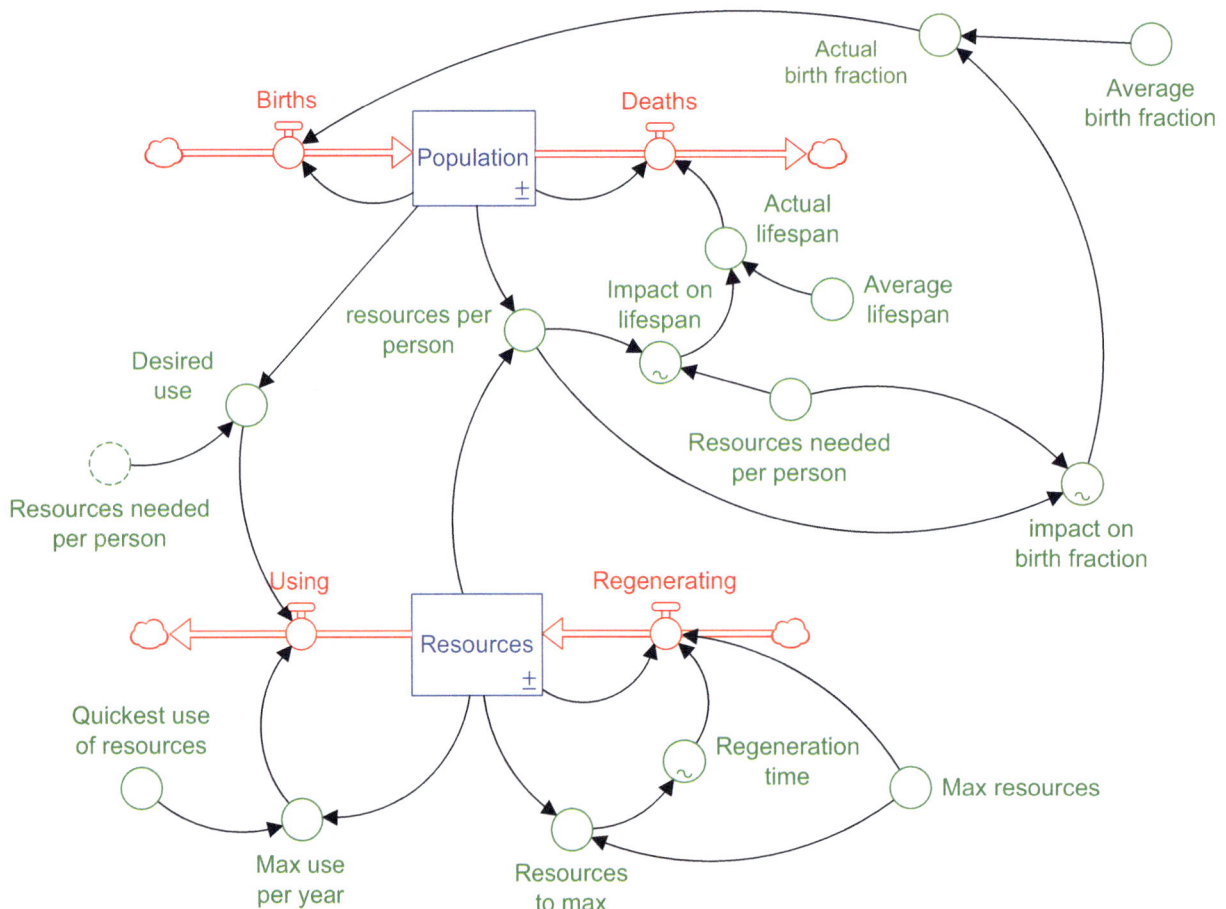

Equations added or changed:
Births = Population*Actual_birth_fraction
Actual_birth_fraction = Average_birth_fraction*impact_on_birth_fraction
Actual_lifespan = Average_lifespan*Impact_on_lifespan
Average_birth_fraction = .02
Average_lifespan = 75
impact_on_birth_fraction = GRAPH(resources_per_person/Resources_needed_per_person)
(0.00, 0.000), (5.00, 0.059), (10.00, 0.204), (15.00, 0.355), (20.00, 0.502), (25.00, 0.640), (30.00, 0.771), (35.00, 0.880), (40.00, 0.955), (45.00, 0.989), (50.00, 1.000)

A real-world example of this type of structure is from China. From 1979-2015, couples in China were generally limited to having just one child. This caused population growth to slow significantly. It also caused some trade-offs that we don't discuss here.

Given the adjustment to this model, the population grows exponentially for awhile, and then levels off at a lower level, a level that the resources can support indefinitely. The key is how you set up the graph for the "Impact on birth fraction."

As of 2015 in China, the population has not yet stabilized. What do you think will happen in China, now that the policy has ended?

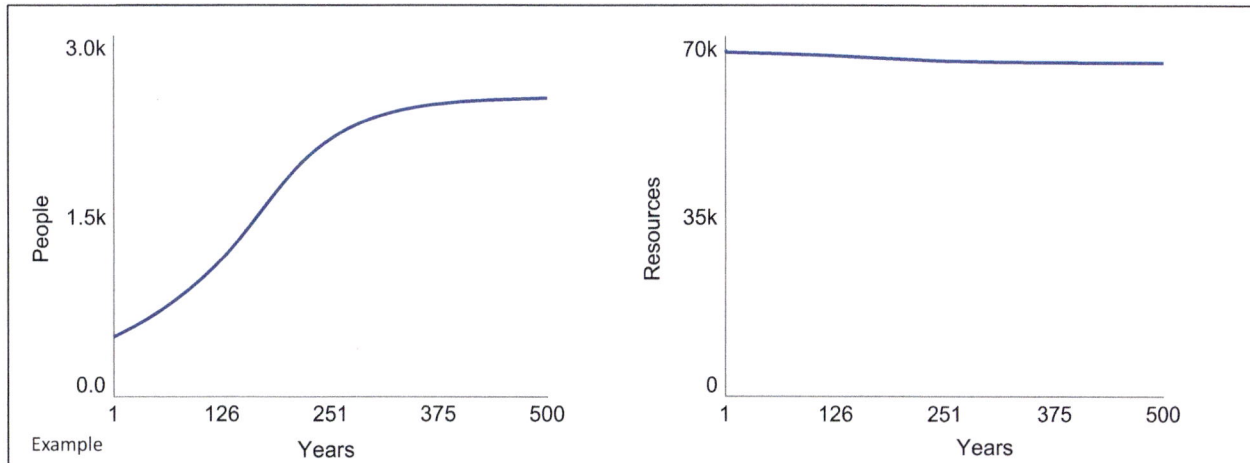

Example

Chapter 6: Stuck in a Rut

Base Model Equations

Deeply_ingrained_habit
   INIT Deeply_ingrained_habit = 100
   INFLOWS:
     Reinforcing_the_habit = (Habit-Deeply_ingrained_habit)/Time_to_change_ingrained_habit
Habit
   INIT Habit = 100
   INFLOWS:
     Ingrained_habit_influencing_behavior = (Deeply_ingrained_habit-Habit)/Time_for_habit_to_influence_behavior
   OUTFLOWS:
     Weakening_habit = Habit*Efforts_to_change_habit
Efforts_to_change_habit = GRAPH(TIME)
(0.00, 0.000), (10.00, 0.000), (20.00, 0.000), (30.00, 0.000), (40.00, 0.000), (50.00, 0.000), (60.00, 0.000)
Time_for_habit_to_influence_behavior = 12
Time_to_change_ingrained_habit = 1E+11

Expected Behavior

Assuming that all equations are entered correctly, you should see no change on the graph as shown.

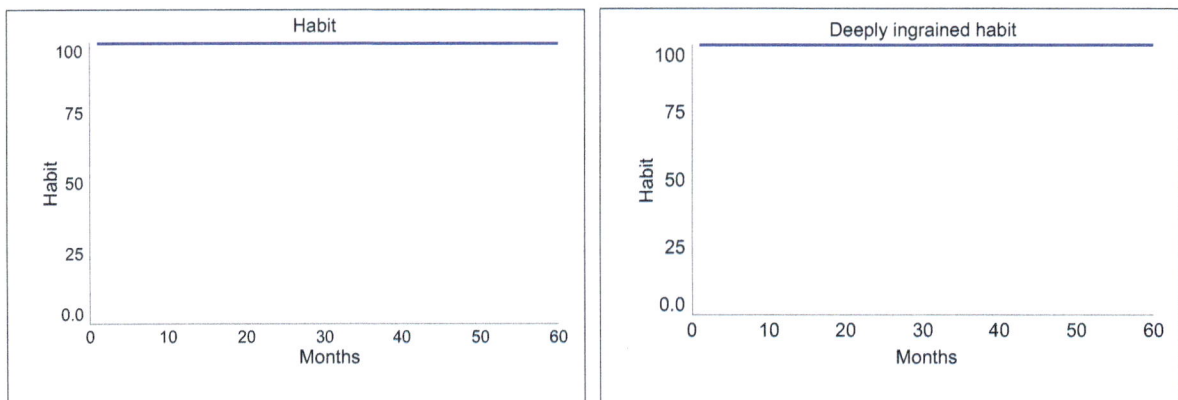

Expected behavior for base model

Troubleshooting

This model's equations are fairly simple, but a couple of factors are important.
1. Make sure that both of the inflows are set to be biflows. Otherwise the habit cannot move in both directions.
2. Check that you have indicated the correct order of operations. Correct placement of parentheses () are important in this model.
3. In the variables that require division, check what is being divided by what.

Base Model - Experiments

Once the model is in equilibrium as shown, the graph for "Efforts to change habit" is adjusted to the following values.

Efforts_to_change_habit = GRAPH(TIME)

(0.00, 0.000), (10.00, 0.000), (20.00, 0.500), (30.00, 0.500), (40.00, 0.000), (50.00, 0.000), (60.00, 0.000)

From there, different settings for the "Time to change ingrained habit" change the results drastically. When it's more difficult to change the deeply ingrained habit, it's much more difficult to change the habit itself. The initial setting of 1E+11, which is 100,000,000,000 indicates that it takes essentially "forever" to reduce a deeply ingrained habit. As a result, people can change a habit in the short term, but rarely change it in the long term. Some habits, like smoking or taking drugs might fall into the "forever" category. Trying shorter settings, such as 36 months and 10 months, shows how it's possible to change a habit if it takes a shorter time to change the deeply ingrained habit.

Dare

The equations for the first dare are exactly the same as the original model, but you'll need to change how long it takes to change the "Time to change ingrained habit" to a number that makes sense for the imagined scenario.

Double Dare

There is no one right answer to this dare, however, one key insight is to realize that habits that are not deeply ingrained are much easier to reduce than those that are deeply ingrained, even when the habit itself starts at a very high level.

Triple Dog Dare

Again, no right answer exists, since each individual's situation would be different. Some key insights include:

1. It's better to eliminate a habit by not starting it in the first place.
2. It's more difficult to eliminate a habit that is deeply ingrained.
3. This model only addresses reducing habits, but doesn't illustrate how to strengthen a desirable habit.

Chapter 7: Fix-it Fun

Challenge 1: The Hatfields and the McCoys

Base Model Equations

Hatfields
   INIT Hatfields = 900
   OUTFLOWS:
      Hatfields_killed_by_McCoys = McCoys*Hatfields_shot_per_McCoy
McCoys
   INIT McCoys = 1000
   OUTFLOWS:
      McCoys_killed_by_Hatfield = Hatfields*McCoys_shot_per_Hatfield
Hatfields_shot_per_McCoy = .2
McCoys_shot_per_Hatfield = .2

Fixed Model and Equations

Notice in the model diagram that two new loops were added to fix the problem of producing a negative population. These two loops are needed to show that the numbers of Hatfields or McCoys shot is dependent on how many of them there are in the respective stocks. If the McCoys are all gone, then none can be shot.

Hatfields
   INIT Hatfields = 900
   OUTFLOWS:
      Hatfields_killed_by_McCoys = McCoys*Hatfields_shot_per_McCoy
McCoys
   INIT McCoys = 1000
   OUTFLOWS:
      McCoys_killed_by_Hatfields = Hatfields*McCoys_shot_per_Hatfield
Hatfields_shot_per_McCoy = GRAPH(Hatfields)
(0, 0.000), (100, 0.000), (200, 0.257), (300, 0.411), (400, 0.543), (500, 0.697), (600, 0.863), (700, 0.931), (800, 1.000), (900, 1.000), (1000, 1.000)
McCoys_shot_per_Hatfield = GRAPH(McCoys)
(0, 0.000), (100, 0.160), (200, 0.383), (300, 0.497), (400, 0.680), (500, 0.771), (600, 0.834), (700, 0.954), (800, 1.000), (900, 1.000), (1000, 1.000)

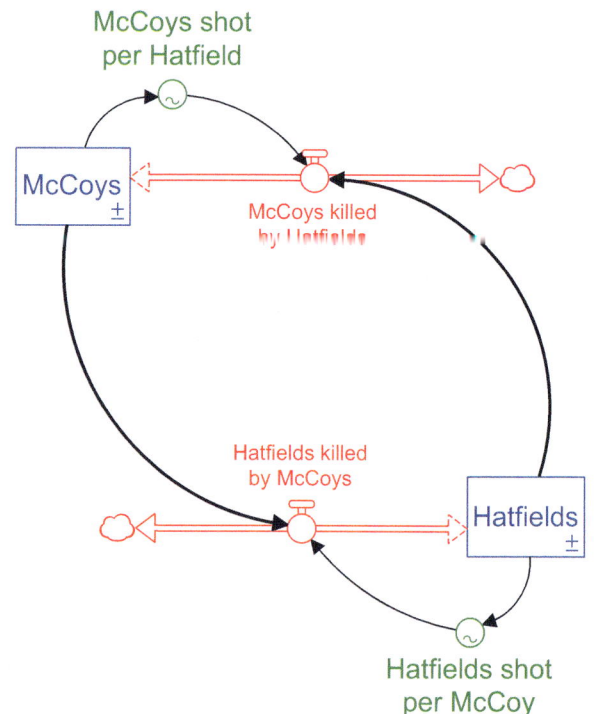

Challenge 2:

Base Model Equations
Households_with_internet
   INIT Households_with_internet = 54600000
   INFLOWS:
     Sign_ups = Sign_ups_from_contacts+Sign_ups_from_ads
Households_without_internet
   INIT Households_without_internet = 54600000
   OUTFLOWS:
     Sign_ups = Sign_ups_from_contacts+Sign_ups_from_ads
Total_US_households
   INIT Total_US_households = Households_without_internet+Households_with_internet
Contacts_per_household_per_year = 2
Fraction_of_households_that_will_never_get_internet = .25
Fraction_with_internet = Households_with_internet/Total_US_households
Fraction_without_internet_signing_up_per_year = 0/100
Households_ready_to_get_internet = Households_without_internet-Households_that_will_never_have_internet
Households_that_will_never_have_internet = Fraction_of_households_that_will_never_get_internet*Total_US_households
Internet_household_data = GRAPH(TIME)
(1984.00, 0.0), (1985.00, 0.0), (1986.00, 0.6), (1987.00, 1.7), (1988.00, 3.0), (1989.00, 3.5), (1990.00, 4.0), (1991.00, 5.0), (1992.00, 6.0), (1993.00, 8.0), (1994.00, 10.0), (1995.00, 13.0), (1996.00, 15.0), (1997.00, 17.0), (1998.00, 18.0), (1999.00, 30.0), (2000.00, 41.5), (2001.00, 45.0), (2002.00, 50.4), (2003.00, 52.0), (2004.00, 54.7), (2005.00, 57.0), (2006.00, 61.7), (2007.00, 68.7), (2008.00, 71.1), (2009.00, 71.3), (2010.00, 71.5), (2011.00, 71.7), (2012.00, 74.8)
Internet_to_non-internet_contacts = Non_internet_contacts_ready_to_sign_up*Fraction_with_internet
Non_internet_contacts_ready_to_sign_up = Households_ready_to_get_internet*Contacts_per_household_per_year
Percent_with_internet = Fraction_with_internet*100
Sign_ups_from_ads = Fraction_without_internet_signing_up_per_year*Households_ready_to_get_internet
Sign_ups_from_contacts = Sign_ups_from_contacts_fraction*Internet_to_non-internet_contacts
Sign_ups_from_contacts_fraction = 5/100

Model's Adjusted Equations
Note that the equations here are just one way to get the model data to closely match the real world data. All equations remain as shown above, except for the ones included here.

Top-Level Model:
Households_with_internet
   INIT Households_with_internet = 0
Households_without_internet
   INIT Households_without_internet = 109200000
Contacts_per_household_per_year = 3.5
Fraction_without_internet_signing_up_per_year = .1/100
Sign_ups_from_contacts_fraction = 15/100

What's interesting to note is that advertising must be greater than zero (0) to get the internet sign ups going. The contacts, though, have great potential for spreading the new idea through a word-of-mouth dynamic. The behavior created by these new settings is shown here.

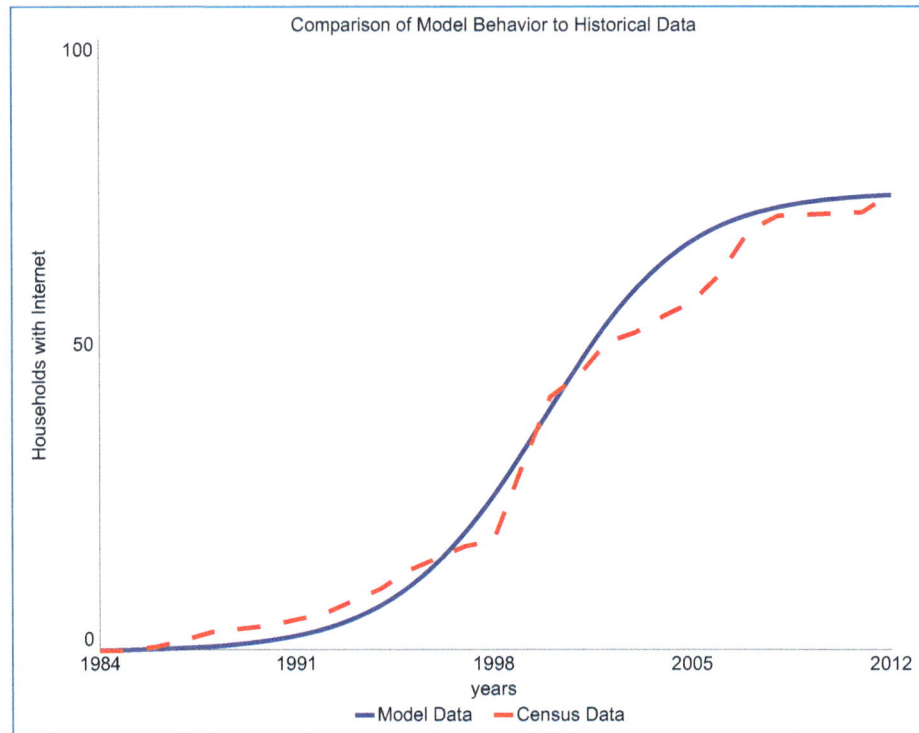

Model data matched to census data

An Explanation of Units

Overview

System dynamics models must always have accurate units in order to have the structure and resulting behaviors make sense. Consider a fruit bowl as an example. It's filled with a variety of fruits, but if we just wanted to count the number of apples, then apples would be our stock with apples going in and apples coming out. I might buy apples at the store and add them to the bowl. I might eat apples and subtract them from the bowl.

I wouldn't go buy oranges, though, and expect that they would add to the number of apples. So for the sake of modeling, as opposed to magic, oranges cannot become apples and peanut butter cannot become jelly.

Fruit Basket, Dirk Ingo Franke, Public Domain

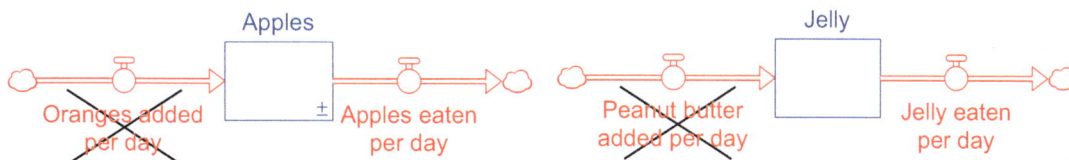

These may seem silly, but novice modelers try to do exactly this in many situations. For example does teaching turn into learning? Teaching can affect learning, but it's a different element, not the same "stuff." Does money turn into ice cream? Of course not. You can use money to buy the ice cream, but it's not a transformation of the money.

An explanation of units at their simplest is, what's in the stock is the same as what's in the connected flow. The stock is the amount of "stuff" while the flow is how much of that same "stuff" goes in or out. Simply speaking, the net change of the stock of Apples = Apples added − Apples eaten.

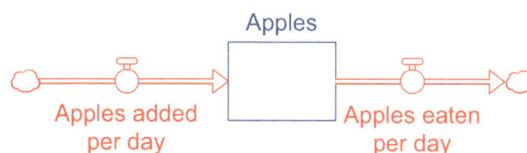

So apples go in, apples accumulate (as a stock), and apples go out. The oranges are nowhere in sight! This principle applies every time an arrow connects parts of a system. All the parts that connect to one another must have logical units, otherwise you'll be creating magic rather than representing how a system really works.

Mathematics plays a crucial role in the way we identify and manage units while modeling. Simple math equations showing connected model elements help determine whether or not a model's units make sense. Each of the following examples shows how the elements' units cancel each other out in such a way that the flows contain the same "stuff" as the stocks. Take a look at each one and then try to solve one on your own. Most modeling software is set up for the user to enter units. Some will even check the units you enter and let you know if you have any errors. If possible, use the software as you look at and then work to enter units into your own models.

Examples

Chapter 2's Energy Drink Model

This model shows how drinking high-caffeine beverages affects caffeine in the body.

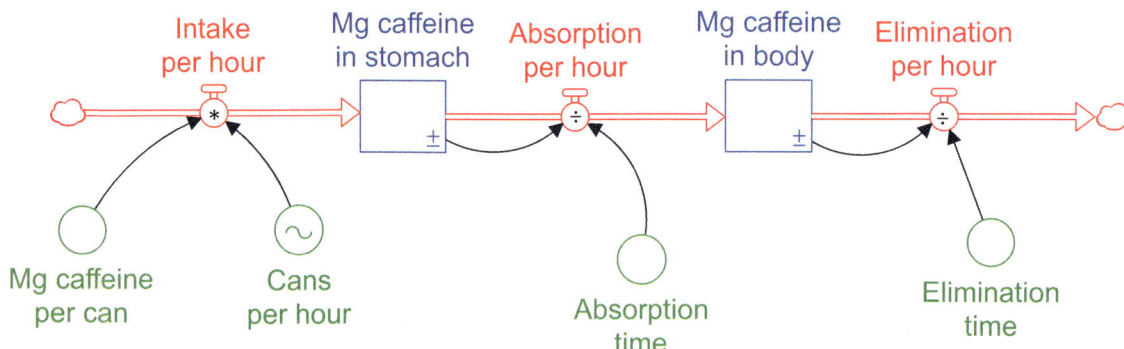

The unit in both stocks is "Mg caffeine."

Flow of "Intake per hour"

$$\frac{Mg\ caffeine}{can} * \frac{Cans}{hour} = \frac{Intake\ (in\ Mg\ caffeine)}{hour}$$

This works because the "Cans" cancel out in the equation.

$$\frac{Mg\ caffeine}{\cancel{can}} * \frac{\cancel{Cans}}{hour} = \frac{Intake\ (in\ Mg\ caffeine)}{hour}$$

Units for the flow of "Intake per hour" makes sense, since caffeine is accumulating as the stock. Remember, flows are always rates (amount per time) and stocks are always the stuff (the amount). What's even cooler is that when the model runs, the time cancels out, and only the stuff gets added (or subtracted) from the stock. You don't have to worry about that part, though. The software handles that equation.

Flow of "Absorption per hour"

$$Mg\ caffeine \div Absorption\ time\ (as\ hours) = \frac{Absorption\ (of\ Mg\ caffeine)}{hour}$$

Again, units for the flow of "Absorption per hour" make sense, since caffeine is accumulating as the stock.

Flow of "Elimination per hour"

What is the equation for the flow? Do the units make sense?

Chapter 3's Goal Model

This model shows how drinking high-caffeine beverages affects caffeine in the body.

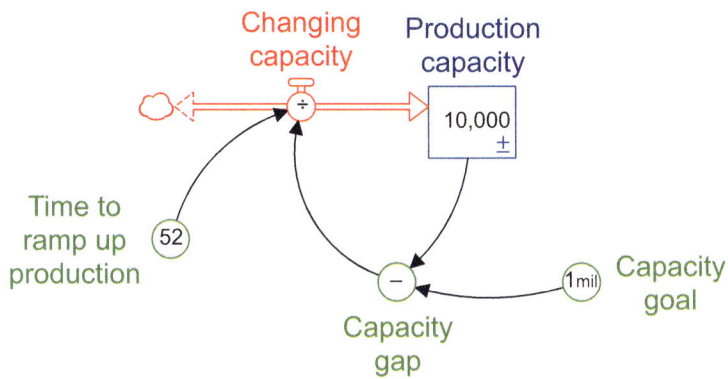

Changing capacity   Production capacity

÷   10,000 ±

Time to ramp up production   52

Capacity gap   −   1mil   Capacity goal

The unit in the stock is devices.

Capacity gap

Capacity goal (devices) – Production capacity (devices) = Capacity gap (devices)

The units for the variable "Capacity gap" makes sense.

Flow of "Changing capacity"

$$\frac{\text{Capacity gap (devices)}}{\text{Time to ramp up production (in weeks)}} = \text{Changing capacity (devices per week)}$$

The units for "Changing capacity" make sense, since the number of devices are accumulating in the stock.

Note that the discussion here is a very brief and simplified summary of the topic of Units.

Chapter 4's Social Media Model

This model shows how ideas can spread in a manner similar to an infection.

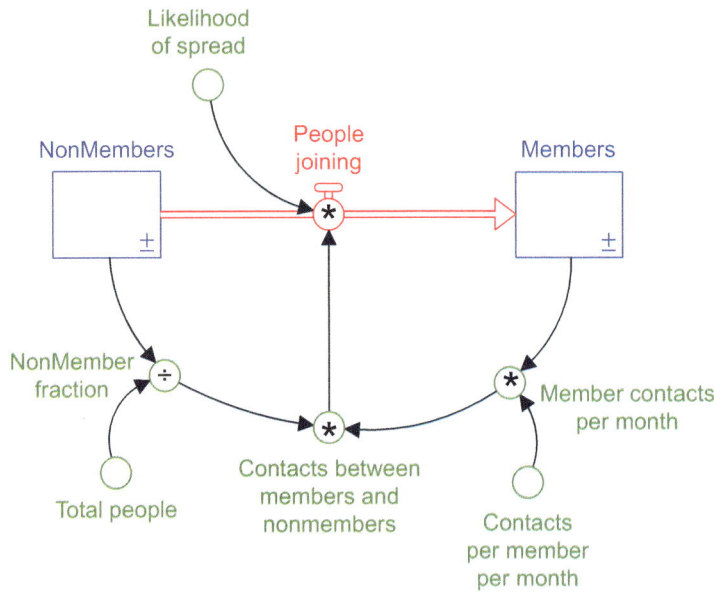

Now it's your turn. Can you figure out the units and whether they make sense for this model? To help you get started, the basic units used in this model are:

- People
- Months
- Contacts
- Dimensionless

  This happens when you have units cancel out completely. For example, the "NonMember fraction" is dimensionless because "NonMembers (which are People) ÷ "Total people" (which are also People) cancels out.

Choose your own model(s)

Choose any model to calculate and check the units. Keep in mind that no matter how complex, the model's units must create a situation in which the "stuff" of the stock is the same as its flows.

Sources

Images
Cover Art
Aurora, Retrieved 2016 from http://www.nasa.gov/mission_pages/station/multimedia/gallery/iss030e102292.html. Public Domain.

Preface
Alston, Dean. Reclinus Maximus [Digital image]. The West Australian. Retrieved 2016 from http://www.airlineratings.com/news/363/our-passengers-who-make-your-flight-hell-survey-results. used with permission.

Jay Forrester, Image from the Creative Learning website, Retrieved 2017 from http://static.clexchange.org/ftp/newsletter/CLEx26.1.pdf#page=1

Getting Started (and throughout)
Bison, U.S Fish & Wildlife, Retrieved 2016 from https://commons.wikimedia.org/wiki/File:Bison_herd_grazing_at_the_National_Bison_Range.jpg. Public Domain

Connections icon, The Iconfactory, Freeware Non-commercial.

Earth from Apollo 17, NASA, Retrieved 2016 from https://commons.wikimedia.org/wiki/File:The_Earth_seen_from_Apollo_17_with_transparent_background.png Public Domain

Giffre River. Retrieved 2016 from https://upload.wikimedia.org/wikipedia/commons/2/2c/Rapids_on_Giffre_river_%28Samoens%29.jpg. Public Domain.

Penguin diver icon. SocialMediaDigger. Retrieved 2016 from Findicons.com.

Planting tree. NASA. Retrieved 2016 from https://commons.wikimedia.org/wiki/File:Jsc2007e048366.jpg. Public Domain.

Puzzle piece icon. Jack Cal. Retrieved 2016 from Findicons.com. Creative Commons, No Attribution.

Shovel icon. Rokey. Retrieved 2016 from Findicons.com. Freeware Non-commercial.

Sunset Hopping, by Reebs, Retrieved 2016 from https://commons.wikimedia.org/wiki/File:Sunset_Hopping.jpg CC 2.0

Chapter 1

Chickens. Retrieved from https://commons.wikimedia.org/wiki/File:20150203Hockenheim07.jpg. Creative Commons Public Domain. [modified]

Dodo, Christian Friedrich Stölze, Retrieved 2016 from https://commons.wikimedia.org/wiki/File:Dodo_stoelzel.jpg, Public Domain

Graduation. Wikimedia Commons. Retrieved from https://commons.wikimedia.org/wiki/File:Unacademic_graduate_HEC_Paris.jpg. Public Domain.

National Debt sign. Jesper Rautell Balle. Retrieved 2016 from https://commons.wikimedia.org/wiki/File:US_National_Debt.jpg. Creative Commons 3.0

Chapter 2

Energy Drink Cans. Mark John Merry. Retrieved 2016 from https://commons.wikimedia.org/wiki/File:Energy_drink_can_art.jpg. Creative Commons 2.0 [modified]

Forest. Jon Sullivan. Retrieved 2016 from https://commons.wikimedia.org/wiki/File:Meadows_trees_grasses_pines.jpg. Public Domain.

Sheep. Retrieved 2016 from http://www.public-domain-image.com/free-images/fauna-animals/sheeps/black-headed-sheep/attachment/black-headed-sheep. Public Domain.

Taking a Pulse. Amanda Mills. USCDCP. Retrieved 2016 from http://www.public-domain-image.com/free-images/science/medical-science/pulse-rate-determined-by-doctor. Public Domain.

Chapter 3

Grade image. Anne LaVigne.

Guitar Frets. Tom Gally. Retrieved 2016 from https://commons.wikimedia.org/wiki/File:Frets,_guitar_neck,_C-major_chord.jpg. Public Domain.

Painting. Pierneef. J.H. in Wêreldspektrum. 1983 Ensiklopedie Afrikana. Public Domain.

Runner. Retrieved 2016 from https://commons.wikimedia.org/wiki/File:Runner_over_blank_map.svg. Public Domain.

Chapter 4

Futuristic Architecture. Steve Maleny. Retrieved 2016 from https://www.flickr.com/photos/maleny_steve/2909480660. Steve Maleny. Creative Commons 2.0.

Lunar Base. NASA. Retrieved 2016 from https://commons.wikimedia.org/wiki/File:Lunar_Base-1.jpg. Public Domain.

Social Media Tree. Retrieved 2016 from https://pixabay.com/en/tree-social-media-structure-1148032/. Creative Commons Public Domain.

The Whisper. ©Malcolm Campbell. sculpture by Andre Wallace. Retrieved 2016 from http://www.geograph.org.uk/more.php?id=2752764. Creative Commmons 2.0.

Chapter 5
Earth from Apollo 17, NASA, Retrieved 2016 from https://commons.wikimedia.org/wiki/File:The_Earth_seen_from_Apollo_17_with_transparent_background.png Public Domain

Moai, A. Urbina, Retrieved 2016 from https://commons.wikimedia.org/wiki/File:Moai_Rano_raraku.jpg Public Domain

Temple, C.T. Liotta, Retrieved 2016 from https://commons.wikimedia.org/wiki/File:Temple_Pyramid_at_Chacchoben.JPG Public Domain

The Twice Lost Tomb, "An All American Architecture," Retrieved from https://commons.wikimedia.org/wiki/File:Architect_and_engineer_(1933)_(14779404044).jpg Public Domain

Chapter 6
Shopping for Groceries, National Archives and Records Administration, Retrieved 2016 from https://commons.wikimedia.org/wiki/File:SHOPPING_FOR_GROCERIES_IN_A_WASHINGTON,_DISTRICT_OF_COLUMBIA_SUPERMARKET_-_NARA_-_555652.jpg, Public Domain.

Runner, U.S. Air Force, Retrieved 2016 from https://upload.wikimedia.org/wikipedia/commons/f/f4/151217-F-SN926-224_%2823611702240%29.jpg, Public Domain.

Stuck in a Rut, ©Charpener, Retrieved 2016 from http://charpener.deviantart.com/art/Stuck-in-a-Rut-527480514 Used with permission

Chapter 7
Consumption Spreads Faster Today graph, Nicholas Felton, used with permission.

Hatfield Clan, Retrieved from https://commons.wikimedia.org/wiki/File:HatfieldClan.jpg, Public Domain.

Hiker, Tinus Badenhorst, Retrieved 2017 from https://commons.wikimedia.org/wiki/File:RolfonteinUitstappiePICT0025.JPG Creative Commons Attribution 3.0 Unported

Man Changing Light statue in Lodz, Guillaume Speurt, Retrieved 2016 from https://commons.wikimedia.org/wiki/File:Man_changing_light_statue_Lodz_(7993535876).jpg Creative Commmons 2.0

Chapter 8
Horse Looking for a Path, Anne LaVigne

Appendix A
Icons from isee systems, inc., used with permission.

Appendix B
Fruit Basket, Dirk Ingo Franke, Retrieved 2017 from https://commons.wikimedia.org/wiki/File:Fruit_basket_alessi.JPG Public Domain.

Websites

Information for Chapter 2 was obtained from the following sources:

Caffeine Informer at:

http://www.caffeineinformer.com/the-half-life-of-caffeine

http://www.caffeineinformer.com/the-caffeine-database

http://www.caffeineinformer.com/caffeine-safe-limits

http://www.caffeineinformer.com/a-real-life-death-by-caffeine

For additional information about energy drink consumption and its effects, see the National Center for Biotechnology Information, http://www.ncbi.nlm.nih.gov/pmc/articles/PMC2966367

About Us

Anne LaVigne

Anne currently works with the Creative Learning Exchange. Her past work includes collaborations with local school districts, a county educational office, and non-profit organizations. For more years than she can count on six hands, she has worked globally alongside educators and students across PK-12 settings using systems thinking and system dynamics tools. She strives to develop and share strategies for understanding dynamic, interdependent systems in ways that empower, engage, and motivate. She co-authored various other resources, including books and lessons, most of which are available through the Creative Learning Exchange. When she isn't exploring dynamic systems, she's a gardener, artist, cheesemaker, and farmer. She loves to hang out with her family in her three-generational household, along with a menagerie of critters including horses, pigs, and cows.

Lees Stuntz

Lees has worked for more than thirty years encouraging the use of system dynamics and systems thinking in K-12 education. As Executive Director of the Creative Learning Exchange, she has created or edited multiple pieces of curriculum – available on the Creative Learning Exchange's website (http://www.clexchange.org), including ten books and numerous curricular units. She collaborates with educators, system dynamicists and citizen advocates toward a collective goal of educating students to be effective systems citizens in our complex world.

The Creative Learning Exchange

The Creative Learning Exchange (CLE) was founded as a non-profit organization in 1991 to encourage an active, learner-centered process of discovery for 5–19 year old students that engages in meaningful, real-world problem solving through the mastery of systems thinking and system dynamics modeling. Since its inception, the CLE has worked to encourage teachers and educators to use systems thinking and system dynamics in classrooms and schools throughout the United States and internationally. The CLE has done this through its website that offers free curriculum and its products that include books and games that promote systems thinking to help educators and students learn and utilize systems thinking and system dynamics in the classroom and the school organization. The CLE also continues to collaborate with individuals and organizations that share our vision of encouraging systems citizenship.

Other Publications by The Creative Learning Exchange

These are just some of the additional resources available from The Creative Learning Exchange to explore how systems work and possible ways to improve them.

CLE Products

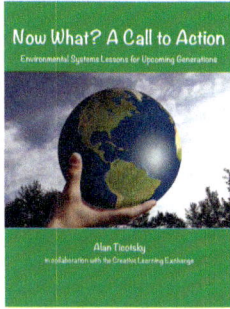

**Now What?
Environmental Systems
Lessons for Upcoming
Generations**

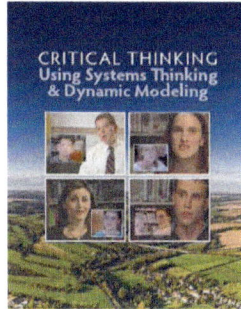

**Critical Thinking
Using Systems Thinking and
Dynamic Modeling**

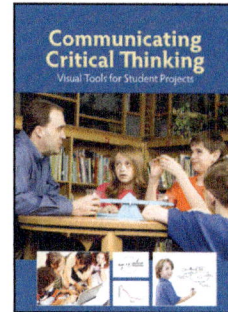

**Communicating Critical
Thinking: Visual Tools for
Student Projects**

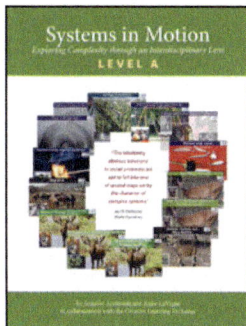

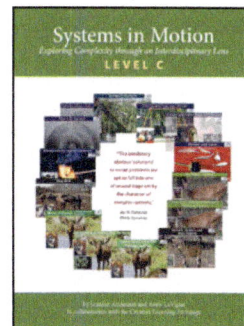

Systems in Motion - Level A, Level B and Level C

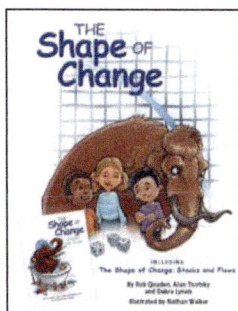

The Shape of Change

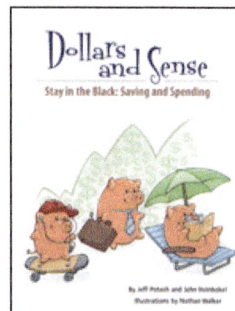

Dollars and Sense I and II

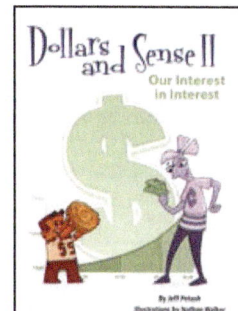

Printed in Great Britain
by Amazon